FROM THE FISHOUSE

FROM THE FISHOUSE

An Anthology of Poems that Sing,
Rhyme, Resound, Syncopate, Alliterate,
and Just Plain Sound Great

**Edited by
Camille T. Dungy, Matt O'Donnell,
and Jeffrey Thomson**

A KAREN & MICHAEL BRAZILLER BOOK
PERSEA BOOKS / NEW YORK

Persea Books, Inc.
853 Broadway
New York, NY 10003

Library of Congress Cataloging-in-Publication Data
From the Fishouse: an anthology of poems that sing, rhyme, resound,
syncopate, alliterate, and just plain sound great / edited by Camille T. Dungy,
Matt O'Donnell, & Jeffrey Thomson.
    p. cm.
"A Karen & Michael Braziller Book."
Includes index.
ISBN 978-0-89255-348-8 (pbk. : alk. paper)
1. American poetry—21st century. I. Dungy, Camille T., 1972– II. O'Donnell,
Matt. III. Thomson, Jeffrey. IV. From the Fishouse
(Organization) V. Title.

    PS617.F75 2009
    811'.608—dc22

2008045403

Printed in the United States of America
Designed by Rita Lascaro

First Edition

"The *sound* is the gold in the ore."
—Robert Frost

CONTENTS

I

To Whoever Set My Truck on Fire:
Poems that Make Various Sorts of Address

II

Alexander Leaves Babylon:
Poems that Tell Other People's Stories

III

A Splinter Becoming a Burning Plank: Poems Disguised as Short Stories, Condensed Novels, and Movie Treatments

IV

Late Twentieth Century in the Form of Litany: Poems that Use Repetition Very Very Well

V

Spangling the Sea: Poems with Convincing
Consonance and Chimes of Internal Rhyme

VI

Understanding Al Green: Poems Written to Music

VII

Cleopatra's Bra: Poems about the Body, the Bawdy, the Sensual, and the Sexy

VIII

Death and *Taxus*: Poems Serious about Puns and Word Play

IX

In the Romantic Longhand of the Night: Formal and Informal Uses of Poetic Form

X

Self-Portrait with Sadness, Wild Turkey, and Denis Johnson: Aubades, Elegies, Odes, and Other Traditional Modes

PLAYLIST OF POEMS
on Accompanying Compact Disc ⓒᴅ

FOREWORD

Plain Talk by Gerald Stern

I have a friend, somewhat cold and classical and a little oppressive, who is fond of saying that in any given period (maybe it was any given decade) there are—say in America—only a given number of true poets—I think it was six. Well, he's cold and classical. And oppressive. And certainly pedantic. From the point of view of quantity alone there are, at a given moment, countless new poets I've never heard of before—and I tend to think of myself as an aficionado of the emerging generations. But it's not just a matter of quantity. There is currently an explosion of poetry that I am delighted by. In fact, even my cold and classical friend might, under the present circumstances, raise the ante a little—could the number of true poets be seven, or even nine?

There are in fact 91 poets in this new anthology alone. These poets have all been published on the *From the Fishouse* Web site, and reflect the taste, of course, of the editors. But what seems to distinguish them, or what is a common, if unwritten, or even unpronounced, emphasis, or focus, of this group of poets is their commitment to the aural and their opposition to the hierarchical or the academic. As such, their poems, more often than not, are comprehensible. They desire to be understood; they desire to be read aloud; they are against obscurity for its own sake. If there are 91 poets here, there is then a generous variety of strategies (use of forms, subjects and such), though I do not mean to imply a movement, a school, a common aesthetic even. I am talking about a tendency, and that only, the result of a series of separate situations: political, poetic, ethnic, aesthetic. And I am observing, and applauding, what, from my distance, seems like a kind of unity.

This is not to say, when I refer to aurality and comprehension, that the poems lack complexity or are, in some way, "written down"; or don't take full advantage of the language and put the poet to the extreme test. The poets in this anthology are courageous and risk-taking; the language is lovely, the poems well-made, the wisdom already there—one doesn't have to wait for it for decades. But throughout this book, I am struck by the use of idiom and the cadences of ordinary American speech: plain talk. Plain talk, even in the most difficult or obscure of poets—for "plain talk," as a poetic term, if you will, doesn't mean simplicity in the usual sense of that word—has been, especially in the twentieth and now twenty-first centuries, the stock-in-trade and the true *disideratum* of every poet who has come up for air, and not only Frost and Williams, but Pound and Stevens as well, and yes, Hart Crane. Plain talk, the utilization (not necessarily celebration) of the colloquial, has philosophical, political, educational, racial, ethnic, economic, and geographical implications, not only poetic ones. It is historically connected with, but not determined by, academic and formal considerations (i.e., considerations of form). It has to do—always—with inclusiveness and, I believe, the destruction, the abnegation, of the priestly—weren't the songs and sermons of both Moses and Jesus, not to mention the prophets, a part of this? Wasn't the audience ordinary and the speech plain?

But each new generation must find its own plain speech, since what is given becomes at last priestly—and ossified. How welcome then these writers, their speech and their concerns. Finally, though, it is something subtle for the subjects are familiar, the subjects as such. If there is a poem in this collection (by Ross Gay) where a young person helps an older one, even in his dying, we after all experienced that in *The Iliad*; and if there is a poem (by Ilya Kaminsky) where war is ridiculed and the ridiculous heroic is exposed, we after all experienced that over and over again, in the last twenty or thirty wars, though perhaps nowhere so acutely and pathetically as in Iraq II, where the foolish cock-of-the-walk King-President urged us to buy (till we drop) as our contribution to the war, to the "war-effort," as we used to say, beautifully realized in one of these poems. The subjects are grief, politics, war, sex, work, jazz, memory, as the subjects were before, but with new voices. The language makes them different: language as it reflects history. So it is the history that is different, or somewhat so; the history that produces these poems.

I don't know at what point a more or less urban—or urban-conditioned—group of poets rose, at ease with the common language, and with a kind of new, commonly realized, or even democratic experience. But this generation—these poets—embody it with a vengeance. It's a delicate point, and it has to do with plunging into the language without self-consciousness. My—hazardous—guess is that it was the generation of Rich, Levine, Merwin, Creeley, Ginsberg, Ashbery—as it happens, my generation—that first was absolutely at ease with the colloquial—neither Williams nor Pound, on the one hand, nor Lowell and Bishop, though one generation derived keenly from the former. There is one poem here (by Steve Scafidi) that is comfortable not only talking about "the hidden crevasses of the body" but the perineum itself—indeed the poem is called "Ode to the Perineum." More than anything else, it is a celebration of the physical, of the body, and takes an extreme position to make its point. I must say that the language is lovely. Nor is shock the purpose or the issue here—I think not—as, say in Ginsberg's asshole songs of yore. There are poems here about holy work (Michael McGriff) or unholy work (Rodger LeGrand) or dull racism (Camille T. Dungy) or East Village nostalgia for Wisconsin (Charles Flowers) or basketball (James Hoch) or Double Dutch (Gregory Pardlo) or the poet cursing (Dan Albergotti) or the poet remembering war (Brian Turner) or gender (Suzanne Wise) or Jazz (Sebastian Matthews) or Blues (Amaud Jamaul Johnson) or divorce (Adrian Blevins) or just plain song (Curtis Bauer).

These poets will be heard from again—and yet again. I praise them for their courage, their audacity, their genius.

Gerald Stern was born in Pittsburgh, Pennsylvania in 1925. He is the author of 15 books of poetry, including, most recently, Save the Last Dance *(Norton, 2008) and* Everything is Burning *(Norton, 2005), as well as* This Time: New and Selected Poems, *which won the 1998 National Book Award, and a book of personal essays,* What I Can't Bear Losing. *He was awarded the 2005 Wallace Stevens Award by the Academy of American Poets and is currently a Chancellor of the Academy of American Poets.*

INTRODUCTION

In the beginning, of course, poetry was completely oral. Poets traveled the country and sang for their supper; they had nothing written down (that idea didn't quite exist yet). They created the poem anew each night around the fire from memorized rhythmic fragments and phrases that the poet strung together in song. Homer's retelling of the *Iliad* or the *Odyssey* was a social event, a unique occurrence never to be repeated exactly the same way again. Lyric poetry emerged with the alphabet, but, like the epic, it was still meant as song, meant to be sung. (Lyric poetry takes its name from the lyre, one of the possible instruments used to accompany poets such as Sappho or Archilocus).

With the rise of literacy and the success of the printing press, poetry moved from a primarily oral art form to one consumed silently. Indeed, we transformed from a culture of listeners to a culture of readers. St. Augustine remarks in his *Confessions* of the astonishment he felt seeing Ambrose reading silently; yet, now, this is something we expect every grade school child to have mastered. And poetry adapted to the new medium, even in its forms.

Nevertheless, poetry retains the power of its oral origins and—it must be noted—not all American poetry has ignored the primacy of the oral tradition. The Beat poets, the Black Arts aesthetic, jazz poetry, the Spoken Word movement: since the mid-twentieth century a number of poetic communities have privileged orality, paying careful attention to the sound of language and the quality of a poem's delivery. Practicing their craft in environments that exposed them to a range of poetics, many of the poets in this collection have been influenced by one or several of these traditions. We've collected in this anthology poetry that combines a number of previously disparate poetic approaches and, doing so, manages to reinvigorate American poetry by giving us new ways to listen.

And listening is one of our (the editors') central concerns. Words matter and how they affect the ear matters. It matters to the way the mind understands and it matters to the way emotions swoon in response to the poem. The texture of words (from the rough edge of Anglo-Saxon to the glide of French and Italian to the syncopation of Black vernacular and the juxtapositions of Spanglish), their feel in the mouth and in the ear, the physical sensations they trigger as they are shaped and vocalized and remembered, the architecture of desire they construct in midair, the idiosyncrasies of each particular speaker, the rhythm of inflection and tone that denote a dialect's geography: all this constitutes the magic through which the day-to-day dross of the spoken language is transmuted into the gold of the poem. This activity of the tongue is missing and much missed in the landscape of contemporary American poetry. We, the editors of this volume, hope to put it back.

We've collected here poems by a group of poets who make the experience of reading their poems aloud rewarding because, by and large, they return to poetry's roots as an instrument for music (or acoustics) and storytelling. It is too easy to say, we think, that all the poets of the post- and post-postmodern eras have simply lost the knack for listening. What we have found instead is that there are scores of emerging poets whose work depends on a careful balance of sound and sense. The poets collected here revel in words, their texture and their grain; they luxuriate in the resonance of the well-turned phrase. They savor rhythm and rhyme, the pulse of the poem as it works. They write for the pleasures of the ear as much as for the pleasures of the mind or heart.

Providing poetry to the ear and giving voice to up-and-coming poets were the founding principles of the *Fishhouse*. At the time of its founding in 2004, there were only a handful of places online where one could go to listen to poetry, and none that concentrated on showcasing the work of emerging poets (defined for the project as those with fewer than two books of published poetry at the time of submission). While audio poetry has proliferated on the Web in the past few years, *Fishhouse* remains the most extensive site of its kind. *Fishhouse* is a resource for poets, fans of poetry, and teachers and students of poetry, and it's a natural extension to collect a sampling of representative poems from the Web site in book form, highlighting the close relationship of the poem text and poetry read aloud, and reminding readers that poetry is *meant* to be read aloud. Focusing attention on the importance of poems in the air was one of the fundamental triggers for *Fishouse*, and showcasing poems that work as well in the air as on the page drives the organization of this collection as well.

We first selected the poems for this anthology by reading and listening to all of the work published (at that point in time) on the *Fishouse* Web site, keeping our ears and eyes open for those poems that, to us, best represented the confluence of sound and sense that *From the Fishouse* represents. As we moved through the process of putting together the anthology, we discovered that many of the poems shared a driving force, a kind of sonic glue that holds the poem together. Some poems chant and echo themselves like mystic songs. Some move more quietly and tell stories that weave and braid themselves into being. Some poems work in and around traditional forms, while others chew their words, as their taste instructs them, to new fashion. Thus our sections evolved, organically, out of the experience of listening to the poems themselves. We should add, however, as Gerald Stern astutely notes in his Foreword, that all these poems share a sense of the aural that transcends the sections. The sections make possible this anthology of poems, but they do not articulate the final meaning for any poem.

The first index cross-references the poems by subcategories of poetic traits. The second index lists the poems and at least three relevant poetic strategies that lead to the success of the poem on the page and out loud. Thus, in our sections, we have grouped poems by a particular technique, while acknowledging (as you might see in the Index of Poetic Traits) that most of the poems assembled here use many or all of these sonic devices.

To build a compelling poem, poets necessarily use many different acoustic techniques, but in any given poem, some techniques will naturally come to dominate. Thus, rather than directly detailing the "proper" application of enjambment or consonance, this collection demonstrates the wonders of the poem, the many components necessary for the creation of sonically engaging poems. Because different poets apply different techniques in various combinations, and because poems so frequently must employ several of these elements simultaneously, we have refrained from grouping the poems too stringently. On the other hand, because readers might want to know a little more about how these poems are working, we have provided the indices as skin-deep points of reference for closer examination of the poems' guts. It is our hope that teachers and readers who are looking for more specific guidance will find these indices useful.

Finally, we have included here an audio sampling of poets reading aloud poems from the anthology, as well as printed excerpts from the poets' responses to questions of craft. We hope these fragments (the full responses being available on the Web site) will bring readers more fully into a conversation with the poems represented here. The accompanying compact disc contains poems from poets with a variety of styles and approaches, but the compilation is by no means the final word. All the poets who appear in this anthology (and many other wonderful poets who do not) are represented on the *From the Fishouse* Web site, and their poems can be heard and savored there: www.fishousepoems.org.

The poems that appear in this anthology show how this new generation of poets is working to create, develop, and nurture the oral aspect of poetry. Each of the poems here represents a passionate attempt to connect sound and sense, to create meaning out of the ineffable puffs of air that leave the human mouth. We celebrate their effort and applaud their accomplishments, but most of all we revel in these voices as they say what must be said.

Camille T. Dungy	Matt O'Donnell	Jeffrey Thomson
San Francisco, California	Pittston, Maine	Farmington, Maine
April 2009		

I

TO WHOEVER SET MY TRUCK ON FIRE
Poems that Make Various Sorts of Address

ANTHONY DEATON

An Early Snow and Winter Comes into Kilter

An early snow and winter comes into kilter.
                        On the tomato vine
                        I seeded too late in summer,
and forgot in its window box,
now no more than a gaunt thrust of green,
one stunted fruit hangs
                        fixed in the glazed
                        clutch of glass on sky
like a lizard in aspic. What to do with it?
So arrives the season of last remains.
                        A lone goose paddles
                        panicked circles in the town's
ice-rimmed pond and will not trumpet into the jet
stream. A mouse
scrabbles around my pantry
                        since the yard went hard
                        with frost.
There's a cat in the road that doesn't move.
                        But isn't this the
                        old song and dance
of the diminished, of the less and less?
How tiring it's become: the seasonal blues and whatnot.
                        Still, I am happy here:
                        day cycles into night,
a single thought in my head:
white snow whitens under moonlight.
                        Dear Reader, rise now
                        and come to my window:
the only one at this hour lit.
I live at the noble end of a poor street.
You'll know it when you see it.
                        Come quickly.
I have something for you.

CHARLOTTE MATTHEWS

To the Men Who Mow the County Graveyards

It won't be long before the designs you form are echoed
in the shivering leaves of an ash tree right there on the hillside

and because it's November those patterns will remain
all winter long, a sort of engraved, emblazoned pattern.

You are walking cautiously and must be able
to read the stones: *Earth hath no sorrow heaven cannot heal.*

Robert Morris, Garland Maupin, Jacob Hall
who just this spring whacked at the bull thistle in his clover field

with a steel scythe, timbre so sheer I held my breath,
as I did, once, under water, because the clang of an anchor

resounded in the heavy sea and my whole body
unwrapped right there in the harbor.

Look back over your shoulder.
The grass is gently sweeping like water at your feet.

It's the same lustrous quiet as the time Robert held
the black string of his dousing pendulum over a plat of land.

At first he whispered, then was wordless, balancing the lead
teardrop between thumb and index finger, letting it sway

and sway in shorter and shorter arcs.
Watching him I felt I'd come a little more alive.

In the dusk somewhere tonight a table lamp comes on.
A woman sits under it recognizing, suddenly, she is all alone.

There is a river moving under all the land.
There never was a night that had no morn.

CATE MARVIN

A Windmill Makes A Statement

You think I like to stand all day, all night,
all any kind of light, to be subject only
to wind? You are right. If seasons undo
me, you are my season. And you are the light
making off with its reflection as my stainless
steel fins spin.
                        On lawns, on lawns we stand,
we windmills make a statement. We turn air,
churn air, turning always on waiting for your
season. There is no lover more lover than the air.
You care, you care as you twist my arms
round, till my songs become popsicle

and I wing out radiants of light all across
suburban lawns. You are right, the churning
is for you, for you are right, no one but you
I spin for all night, all day, restless for your

sight to pass across the lawn, tease grasses,
because I so like how you lay above me,
how I hovered beneath you, and we learned
some other way to say: *There you are.*

You strip the cut, splice it to strips, you mill
the wind, you scissor the air into ecstasy until
all lawns shimmer with your bluest energy.

Cate Marvin on the greatest obstacle to becoming a poet
No one wants you to write, which is why you can't make any money doing
it, and frankly what I like about poetry is that you can't make any money
doing it. It's the one thing that's not a commodity. It's a big fuck you to the
world, really, you know? It's the most crazy, beautiful, extravagant, and necessary thing to do.

LINDSAY AHL
Wolf

Wolf, I saw you down at the shoreline.
I saw you run under the aquaduct.
The rain made it all a blur.

Wolf, I saw you on Sunset Boulevard, the cars swerving,
that night when the horizon stayed orange.
I saw you later in the trash, your eyes yellow, hollowed,
your fur oily, dark—

you probably heard the cello suites from the third
floor. Bach is still alive, but I can tell you he's in a storm too
the notes afire and falling: good, like breathing
in.

        Only later
you might have noticed
or not, with the staleness in the Los Angeles air,
        the ghosts and angels.

Wolf, I see your legs running.
The ocean is vast behind you, boardwalks, the ruins of the carnival,
the voices calling. But you know how to run.

It's all a storm, wolf. I see you only now.

DOBBY GIBSON
Gone Before

Sadness, though your beard may be fake,
your anonymity is quite real,
whispered the dying man to his nurse,
raising his arms for his last sponge bath.
Early renderings had no vanishing point.
Painters dream in oil.
Dreams, like canaries,
are sent down into our mineshafts
to discover how long we might survive;
the dreamers, like secretaries,
are sent home in sneakers,
carrying their pumps.
Sadness, you are so Japanese: snow
on just one side of the leaf
that has not yet dropped.
Snow of all snow
and of every lost chance,
last insects walking in fear across glass,
zeppelin beacons pulsing through the fog.
Snow as illegible as the cardboard
held by the man who can't spell
how hungry he is,
kneeling frozen at the fountain
to sail a small boat
folded from his last dollar.
Seen from deep orbit,
cities wink white with loneliness.
A mother pulls her daughter by her arm.
A little girl pulls her doll by its hair.
Inside the space capsule after splashdown:
no one. And not even a note.
The hospitals they have built
just for people like us to die in
are built entirely of corridors,
which they keep empty,
except for a grinding light.
Outside, the snow falls without making a sound.
And still the dogs scatter.

BRIAN TURNER
Here, Bullet (CD)

If a body is what you want,
then here is bone and gristle and flesh.
Here is the clavicle-snapped wish,
the aorta's opened valves, the leap
thought makes at the synaptic gap.
Here is the adrenaline rush you crave,
that inexorable flight, that insane puncture
into heat and blood. And I dare you to finish
what you've started. Because here, Bullet,
here is where I complete the word you bring
hissing through the air, here is where I moan
the barrel's cold esophagus, triggering
my tongue's explosives for the rifling I have
inside of me, each twist of the round
spun deeper, because here, Bullet,
here is where the world ends, every time.

STEVE SCAFIDI
To Whoever Set My Truck On Fire ⓒ

But let us be friends awhile and understand our differences
are small and that they float like dust in sunny rooms
and let us settle into the good work of being strangers
simply who have something to say in the middle of the night
for you have said something that interests me—something of flames,

footsteps and the hard heavy charge of an engine gunning away
into the June cool of four in the morning here in West Virginia
where last night I woke to the sound of a door slamming,
five or six fading footsteps, and through the window saw
my impossible truck bright orange like a maverick sun and

ran—I did—panicked in my underwear bobbling the dumb
extinguisher too complex it seemed for putting out fires
and so grabbed a skillet and jumped about like one
needing to piss while the faucet like honey issued its slow
sweet water and you I noticed then were watching

from your idling car far enough away I could not make
your plate number but you could see me—half naked
figuring out the puzzle of a fire thirty seconds from
a dream never to be remembered while the local chaos
of a growing fire crackled through the books and boots

burning in my truck, you bastard, you watched as I sprayed
finally the flames with a gardenhose under the moon
and yes I cut what was surely a ridiculous figure there
and worsened it later that morning after the bored police
drove home lazily and I stalked the road in front of my house

with an ax in my hand and walked into the road after
every car to memorize the plates of who might have done this:
LB 7329, NT 7663, and you may have passed by—
I don't know—you may have passed by as I committed
the innocent numbers of neighbors to memory and maybe

you were miles away and I, like the woodsman of fairy tales,
threatened all with my bright ax shining with the evil
joy of vengeance and mad hunger to bring harm—heavy
harm—to the coward who did this and if I find you,
my friend, I promise you I will lay the sharp blade deep

into your body until the humid grabbing hands of what must be
death have mercy and take you away from the constant
murderous swinging my mind makes my words make
swinging down on your body and may your children
weep a thousand tears at your small and bewildered grave.

REB LIVINGSTON
Tonight I Doze

Because insomnia is no fun and who's dark and frilly now?
Not me, yes me, oh woe whoa, what did we step in this time?
Everything was textbook sweetness, tv show thrillingness
and then, then, fuck you and your then, hairy hands
spiral eyeballs, pat and rub, whimsy stick, I saw you
peek-a-wink, yes you simply offered alternatives.
I lapped lipped your radiation, let you sneak in the side
kissed cursed your crooked eyelids, lived loved your false greetings.
Those were good days, those three, they shouldn't have ended but
clocks, they were born to run, hah, I'm trying to be funny.
You made me nervous, bulbous, fortuitous, I'm using big words
and I don't know what they mean. I squealed for ya.
That's what I did and you got sleepy and said now we could sleep.
I didn't want to sleep, I wanted to talk and go back in time
so there'd be nothing to talk about and start over and graze
past, shake hands, shake an ankle, kiss kiss. There was that
stairwell, that lost opportunity of steps and railings.
Now I'm fat, draped in flannel and you take too damn long
to respond and never answer important questions
like . . .

DIANA MARIE DELGADO
Correspondence

Brother, deep in the moth hour and still no altar to speak of.
Everyone's got a life they cannot stop. Time passes, nothing survives.

The real me slipped out like a hiccup and Z marooned
himself in the arms of another girl's couch. *I have a book for you.*

It's about life and a real time G doing it. Mom's fine, breaking
crooked as an eggshell. Dad the same teething crocodile.

I've never seen so much sad architecture. Remember when the field
froze white and Mom tied plastic over our shoes?

This is the only place that's ever felt like home. I hope you get this
letter before lockdown. Or have you learned how to read in the dark?

MARIA HUMMEL

Letter to Cain

I could say certain things and you'd know what I mean: ground that does not sink to the boot—although it is green, although rain falls continuously on it—cold limbs battering the air, and no ice yet.

You'd know what I mean if I said we are between. Between seasons, yes, but also between the moment when you swallow and the meat hits your gut, when you cut skin and the blood wells up.

You'd know to find me here, hanging my arms over the edge of a fence, stirring the grass with my boot to see exactly where the earth still froze.

We have that hardness in us, and it is not just bone.

Our flesh has long resisted melting as the soil will not unclench for the plow, not yet, not now when we want it to but when we've gone past desire and necessity to the place where you cut your brother's heart out just to warm your hands.

Tell me about that place. I think I have seen it, stained at the edges of the field, in the jaw of a dog after he tore a sheep to bits. I reached into his mouth and pulled out the shame that was missing from his eyes.

You'd know what I mean if I said the earth must be torn, if I said some wounds open before the knife even touches the skin.

V. PENELOPE PELIZZON
To Certain Students

On all the days I shut my door to light,
all the nights I turned my mind from sleep

while snow fell, closing the space between the trees
till dawn ran its iron needle through the east,

in order to read the scribblings of your compeers,
illiterate to what Martian sense they made

and mourning my marginalia's failure to move them,
you were what drew me from stupor at the new day's bell.

You with your pink hair and broken heart;
you with your knived smile; you who tried to quit

pre-law for poetry ("my parents would kill me");
you the Philosopher King; you who saw Orpheus

alone at the bar and got him to follow you home; you
green things whose songs could move the oldest tree to tears.

V. Penelope Pelizzon on wrestling with the muse

I'm someone who tends to be very willful and very stubborn in my normal daily life, so when I sit down to write, it's part of the challenge to let language drive the car, drive the engine. To badly paraphrase Auden, your muse gives you things but doesn't expect you to be passive; you have to fight back a little bit. Part of the fun there is to see where it goes, where it takes itself, where it takes the poem, and then to have a productive wrestling match with it.

PAUL GUEST
Questions for Godzilla ⓒ

What of the atom's split heart we made
for you and the godly flash-bang wrath,
the anguished song, the clawed gait,
the zipper by which one of us slips into
and puts you on, your death we dangle
like a carrot, your stunted son mewling
always, your ragged arch foes,
your bed in rock, in magma, in thick sea slime,
our fascination still, our morbid heart,
our scattering like leaves, our blood
that once was horrible, a Technicolor ichor,
what of the glowing spine,
what of the toy stings of stock footage flames,
what of the jets you swatted dead
from the air with unmistakable joy,
you of the plastic-leather, pebbled Pleistocene flesh,
you of the palsied fury, you
of the put-upon by dissemblers and disturbers,
you, what of the life burned
so cheaply into celluloid we are charmed,
what of autumn, what of the earth
we took you from, what of the sky's wounded throb,
the sallow child darkened
in your shadow, what of those thousand fates
cut in coiling ribbons
to the floor, what of the heaven they hoped on
that glowed like your breath,
that sang only before you came,
that fell quiet like a feather,
what of the shouted orders,
the dread retreat, the fall of a world built to scale,
what is pain to you?

OLIVER DE LA PAZ
Hello,

Hello, constellation—my other face
as suburbia explodes at dawn.

Windy hello, my blown-away papers,
    sheets radiating like dandelion seeds.

Hello, silo's gleaming tin saying, *breathe* as I pass along the highway.
    Shiny hello.

Guard at the halfway house disappearing for an hour, hello.
    I missed the light off your sunglasses.

Hello, footfall on sand tilting the earth's axis, its darkening arch.

My blue blanket, childhood bleached in the yard—hello.

My crickets playing their hairs: *tchick tchick*,
    like some dying machine—hello.

Hello, hirsute walking away from the circus tent,
    your eyes flickering in the afternoon like wild butane lighters,

My curtain to a darkroom letting me see a fingernail of red light—
    I think of bathing in hotels. Hello hotels,
    sunshine, and complimentary coffee.

Perfume on a hot day. Hello Cecelia from sixth grade
    who had worn no underwear for Social Studies . . . I was at the
        desk behind you
    when you turned and froze me with your teeth.

Colder than hello, my saxophone—I don't play.

My jazz of hard liquor. My drunk, hello,
    who approaches my car saying, "You are shameless, you are
        shameless."
    Meanwhile, the sunlight off broken glass is everywhere.

Hello shame. Hello and thanks. My devilish . . . with her spiky heels.
   Been long.

Hello sadness, beautiful, beautiful.

Hello, hat on the bed struck by a sunbeam
   serving as a symbol as the rattle of the gravel trucks
   returns you to the world.

Hello again, Cecelia, your mouth shut
   after seeing your lover pour gasoline on his hands. Hello
      hunger.

Hello, my hunger, angry at yourself. Hello, yourself.

Hello to myself who has no moonlight. Moonlight spangled hello.

My God, hello. You left your wallet and your keys. Where are you
   going without them? You can't go far. Not far at all.

KATE NORTHROP
The Film ⓒⅮ

Come, let's go in.
The ticket-taker
has shyly grinned
and it's almost time,
Lovely One.
Let's go in.

The wind tonight's too wild.
The sky too deep,
too thin. Already it's time.
The lights have dimmed.
Come, Loveliest.
Let's go in

and know these bodies
we do not have to own, passing
quietly as dreams, as snow.
Already leaves are falling
and music begins.
Lovely One,

it's time.
Let's go in.

Kate Northrop on memorizing poems
I require all my students to memorize and recite a poem. I don't require this
to strengthen their memory skills. I want them to memorize a poem so they
can come to know one poem intimately, so they can feel in a more physical
sense how the poem takes shape, how the poem turns, and rises and falls,
and rises again. To have a poem memorized that takes shape simply by your
saying it is to have this world available to you at every moment, any moment
of the day. The whole world of poetry that has come before is ours to own,
and to have it inside you to say whenever you want is to realize how big a
gift it is.

II

ALEXANDER LEAVES BABYLON
Poems that Tell Other People's Stories

TINA CHANG

Servitude

Li Sau and Li Jie   [Hunan, 1938]

She takes one breast out of her silken undershirt
like a secret, a warm brown egg and places it into his
open mouth. His body is hammocked

in floral cloth, tied to her bosom. August sweats
at the base of her neck. She gives away
her milk to a child she calls *shiou an*, smallest

night. She wishes he were her own as she crouches
in a field separating rotted stems from dried tea leaves.
I think of unraveling her two long

braids when I do the chores—chasing the crazed
chickens with their throats cut, stringing them by their feet
to the front trees. Bodies dripping

with leaves, the air smells of wild blood everywhere.
Tonight, after she has swept stiff crickets down the back steps,
after I have washed dung from my fingernails with ginger

she will come quietly. We will lie down
on woven straw mats and watch the hanging
branches scrape against the unarmed sky.

She puts her fingers to my lips which smell of
smashed guava and lilac powder. I eat what she
has brought me: bits of pig knuckle and mushrooms

collapsed in brown sauce. The whole town is strewn
with horses and red doorways and burned fish.
Past this house, there is a field which is set afire.

The torching of it like a lit city.
Li Sau, the bruised night pours in through all
the shutters of the house and nothing is coming for us.

RAVI SHANKAR

Sea Watchers, Oil Paint on Canvas, 1952

*"I find in working, always the distracting intrusion of elements not
a part of my most interested vision, and the inevitable obliteration
and replacement of this vision by the work itself as it proceeds."*
                                        —Edward Hopper

Not the Hamptons, even a half-century ago,
more barren in midday than a beach should be,
gull-less, garrulous only on the clothesline
where orange and yellow towels flutter dry.

Impassive as the angular stones in the sand,
husband and wife steep in the sun, silent.
It's been years since they felt any need
for small talk and now, childless, on vacation,

they've chosen a concrete shore house
to spend a week swimming, eating lobster
rolls at the shack in the center of town,
and watching the clear hyaline sea darken

in spots over the kelp-encrusted rocks.
At night, she will undress, carefully folding
her navy blue two-piece swimsuit over
the porcelain lip of the streaked claw-foot

tub that stands adjacent to the narrow bed
where he reclines, reading a *Popular Mechanics*.
She will unhook the clasp of the swim cap
under her chin to shake out her still-damp

hair, to frown fractionally at the mirror
before getting into bed. In a few minutes,
he will place the magazine in the bedside
table's oak drawer, click off the lamp,

and without exchanging a word, hold her
by the ankles to better gain purchase
on the taut cotton sheets she will remake
in the morning when he jogs on the beach.

Ravi Shankar on revision
I think missteps are important. To trust yourself enough to write something
that doesn't really reveal what it is you wish to reveal in a poem can lead to
the next thing you write which in fact can be the right real thing.

TRACY K. SMITH
Mangoes

The woman in a blouse
The color of daylight
Motions to her daughter not to slouch.
They wait without luggage.
They have been waiting
Since before the station smelled
Of cigarettes. Shadows
Fill the doorway and fade
One by one
Into bloated faces.
She'd like to swat at them
Like the lazy flies
That swarm her kitchen.

She considers her hands, at rest
Like pale fruits in her lap. Should she
Gather them in her skirt and hurry
Down the tree in reverse, greedy
For a vivid mouthful of something
Sweet? The sun gets brighter
As it drops low. Soon the room
Will glow gold with late afternoon.
Still no husband, face creased from sleep,
His one bag across his chest. Soon
The windows will grow black. Still
No one with his hand always returning
To the hollow below her back.

Desire is a city of yellow houses
As it surrenders its drunks to the night.
It is the drunks on ancient bicycles
Warbling into motionless air,
And the pigeons, asleep in branches,
That will repeat the same songs tomorrow
Believing them new. Desire is the woman
Awake now over a bowl of ashes
That flutter and drop like abandoned feathers.

It's the word *widow* spelled slowly in air
With a cigarette that burns
On its own going.

Tracy K. Smith on the pleasure and pain of writing

I remember the moment when I learned that a poem could start from something it didn't know the answer to or start from an experience that I didn't fully understand I felt. I remember feeling so relieved. The process of sitting down to write a poem suddenly was really fun. When I get the itch to start something now it's not because of what I know, it's because of what I wonder, and it makes the process so much more satisfying because it's so much more unpredictable. The pain is very deeply connected to the pleasure, and it's about that not knowing. I get an idea for writing a poem and I commit to the first lines and I have that feeling, the exact feeling of falling in love, and then I get scared, and I don't know if the poem is something I'm capable of bringing to its rightful close and I wonder if what I'm able to see and say is adequate for what the poem's promise is.

GREGORY PARDLO
Double Dutch ⓒ

The girls turning double-dutch
bob & weave like boxers pulling
punches, shadowing each other,
sparring across the slack cord
casting parabolas in the air. They
whip quick as an infant's pulse
and the jumper, before she
enters the winking, nods in time
as if she has a notion to share,
waiting her chance to speak. But she's
anticipating the upbeat
like a bandleader counting off
the tune they are about to swing into.
The jumper stair-steps into mid-air
as if she's jumping rope in low-gravity,
training for a lunar mission. Airborne a moment
long enough to fit a second thought in,
she looks caught in the mouth bones of a fish
as she flutter-floats into motion
like a figure in a stack of time-lapse photos
thumbed alive. Once inside,
the bells tied to her shoestrings rouse the gods
who've lain in the dust since the Dutch
acquired Manhattan. How she dances
patterns like a dust-heavy bee retracing
its travels in scale before the hive. How
the whole stunning contraption of girl and rope
slaps and scoops like a paddle boat.
Her misted skin arranges the light
with each adjustment and flex. Now heather-
hued, now sheen, light listing on the fulcrum
of a wrist and the bare jutted joints of elbow
and knee, and the faceted surfaces of muscle,
surfaces fracturing and reforming
like a sun-tickled sleeve of running water.
She makes jewelry of herself and garlands
the ground with shadows.

PATRICK ROSAL

Who Says the Eye Loves Symmetry

For Maureen Clyne

Doesn't the eye love the ragged
tear of sky the treetop-shred
horizon The eye—after all—
loves the dizzy
dip of a road: its precarious
tilt towards a ravine
only wrist-deep water
and giant smooth rocks to break
the sky's fall The eye
loves the bit peach window agape
buildings caught mid-swagger across a skyline
The eye loves unpainted pickets
cracked planks the harlequin the prow
poked out of water
like a chin loves
the evergreen arched over a flood
like an old man looking into the street
for a hand loves a sawed link chewed
rope a birch's slants But
the eye can't
love what it can't
see: the woman
striding tired and brave amid the lobby's bustle
and under her shirt
a single breast

Patrick Rosal with advice to young writers
Read everything you can possibly get your hands on to know what you like,
and to know what you don't like, and *why*.

AMAUD JAMAUL JOHNSON
Burlesque ⊙

Watch the fire undress him,
how flame fingers each button,
rolls back his collar, unzips him
without sweet talk or mystery.

See how the skin begins to gather
at his ankles, how it slips into
the embers, how it shimmers
beneath him, unshapen, iridescent,

as candlelight on a dark negligee.
Come, look at him, at all his goods,
how his whole body becomes song,
an aria of light, a psalm's kaleidoscope.

Listen as he lets loose an opus,
night's national anthem, the tune
you can't name, but can't stop humming.
There, he burns brilliant as a blue note.

SHANE BOOK
The One

The enormous head and huge
bulbed knees, elongated
hands and feet, don't fit
with the filed-down chest, limbs
of kindling, yet this is one
whole boy, suspended
in a cloth harness hooked
to what looks like a clock
stuck at three fifteen.
Closer, you can see it is
not a clock but a scale,
the kind you find in any North
American grocery,
but of course this is not
North America, this is
the Sahel famine, this
is Mali in 1985, where a boy
waiting for his rations
to be adjusted
must be weighed. At once
his face relays one and many
things: he could be crying out,
he could be grinning,
he could be frightened
or tired, he could believe
he is suspended in unending
dream. What starvation started
gravity refines as the boy
reclines, the hunger having
collapsed his neck, his face
staring up at the ceiling
of sticks which like most ceilings
anywhere in this world is blank.

MONICA FERRELL

Alexander Leaves Babylon

*Alexander the Great died of a mysterious fever contracted at a feast
in Babylon. He was there returning from his campaign in India; it had
ended with a disastrous crossing of the Gedrosian desert which grue-
somely decimated his army.*

Alexander wept in Babylon, not because
his father had died or his old tutor
had looked at him finally with those eyes of stone

but because the drink of Babylon
was so good. It tasted of dandelion milk
squeezed from a stalk still in its greenness.

Here in his hand—the world: but first this glass of clarity
swelling like sunlight and as sharp. Yes, winter
had aged him suddenly as a straw statue left outdoors

in the everness of the terrible Gedrosian:
that skin-colored bowl soft as the palm of God
where the urge to understand met the urge to disappear

and the two lay down to couple in the dust.
Sand scrubbed him clean as a glass there; he came out
empty as the strange room that widens between

two heart-beats: vacant as this circle of faces gathered at table—
flames staring quietly from a white fire
visionlessly patient in its dinner of elimination.

I need no one else I am a star
                        Then the gemmed
cats ranged under the table, and a rainbow-
colored snail kissed the marbling foot.

GEOFFREY BROCK

The State of Virginia after Southampton: 1831

And now our nights are spent listening to noises,
he writes to his sister, months after hearing the news.

He recalls turning, as the messenger's dust-trail
drifted north, toward the house his father built,

seeing the blur of his wife moving through the parlor,
his son wrestling the cook's boy on the porch.

From the field came the usual rustle of tools
and voices. *A corn song, a hog call, has often been*

the subject of nervous terror, and a cat in the dining room
will banish sleep for the night. He did not look at the field,

at the dark thin shapes he knew he would find there,
bending and turning—they too would hear the news.

Now, he dips his pen and pauses, wanting to end
with some insight. Picturing her frown, he instead

merely inquires again whether Cincinnati
still agrees with her, and whether they've had snow.

Geoffrey Brock on the genesis of "The State of Virginia . . . "
The spark for the poem came from a letter written by a white Virginia farmer
to someone in Cincinnati several months after Nat Turner's rebellion. I'm
fond in general of reading the letters and diaries of ordinary people who were
minor participants in or witnesses to historical events. In such documents I
often find an immediacy, an unfiltered quality, that is rarely present in the
history books or in the writings of more famous people. I was particularly
drawn to this letter for several reasons: the restraint, the indirection with
which it's written. And, of course, the language of it appealed to me. "Corn
song," for example. I still don't know exactly what that means, to be honest,
but I love the sound of it, especially followed immediately by "hog call."

KYLE G. DARGAN
The Battlefield

for Darrell Burton

That night a mantle of snow fell over all of the bodies, sharp
and fine like sky grating itself. Limbs twice brittle, cold on
corpus morta, sunk while ground and horizon grew
to touch each other. Five months, the icy shards fell like one name,
cataloguing every breathless man as one casualty. It dissolved
with their flesh and seeped into the pores beneath the grass.

Widows flocked to the wells, to the rivers—scooping hands and
     buckets,
shoes and skirt bottoms. Each poured what they gathered
into wooden bowls, flexed forearms with the alchemy of making
dough they'd feed to pear-shaped kilns. When the bread had baked,
they gathered all the daughters, made them watch while the boys ate.

Kyle G. Dargan on his writing time
I've probably written my most, at least to me, interesting poems, or at least
got the start for them, while I was on public transportation.

SARAH LINDSAY

Cheese Penguin

The world is large and full of ice;
it is hard to amaze. Its attention
may take the form of sea leopards.
That much any penguin knows
that staggers onto Cape Royds in the spring.
They bark, they bow one to another,
she swans forward, he walks on her back,
they get on with it. Later
he assumes his post, an egg between his ankles.

Explorers want to see everything, even
the faces of penguins whose eggs have been stolen
for science. At night they close the tent flaps
to fabricate sundown, hunch together
over penguin fried in butter, and write up their notes.
Mornings they clump over shit-stained rocks,
tuck eggs in their mittens, and shout.
Got one, got one. They shove back their balaclavas;
they feel warm all over.

The penguins scurry for something to mother,
anyone's egg will do, any egg
no matter how stiff and useless the contents,
even an egg-shaped stone to warm—
and one observer slips to a widow
a red tin that once held cheese.
Finally the wooden ship sails, full of salted penguin,
dozens of notebooks, embryos,
explorers who missed as little as possible. But:

The penguin cherished the red tin on her feet.
She knew what was meant to happen next
and she wanted it, with a pure desire
refined for thirty-five million years
in the dark eye of every progenitive cell.

And it happened. A red tin beak broke through
and a baby flopped into the rock nest, smelling of cheese—
but soon he was covered with guano, so that was all right.
Begging for krill from his aunts' throats just like the others.

Winter: blue ice, green ice, black sea,
hot breath of yellow-jawed killer whales.
Summer: pink slime on black rock,
skuas that aim for the eye. Krill, krill,
a shivering molt, krill, krill, a mate,
and so on. And though he craved dairy products
he never found any; though he was miraculous
no one came to say so. The world is large,
and without a fuss has absorbed stranger things than this.

JAMES HOCH

Late Autumn Wasp

One must admire the desperate way
       it flings
itself through air amid winter's slow
       paralysis,

and clings to shriveled fruit, dropped
       Coke bottle,
any sugary residue, any unctuous
       carcass,

and slug-drunk grows stiff, its joints
       unswiveled,
wings stale and oar-still, like a heart;
       yes, almost

too easily like a heart the way, cudgeled,
       it lies
waiting for shift of season, light, a thing
       to drink down,

gnaw on, or, failing that, leaves half of
       itself torn
willingly, ever-quivering, in some
       larger figure.

James Hoch on the importance of poetry

If there is an argument for universality of human kind, it must be poetry's business. It must be evidence of the ability to move across time and geography, across gender, and experience in order to find an empathy via the imagination. I think that's what poetry gives the world.

DAVID RODERICK
Colony

First the sea came true
        and then the land because the bones
of their followers
found hard earth,
        foothold and roothold,
pine-pitch stains on their clothes.

        Clouds memorized them
and moved on,
        cool shadows pulled by a pagan wind.

        Because *every false doctrine*
stingeth like a viper,
        they built a gun-port and fort,
a row of lathed pews,
and when phlegm
        rattled in their preacher's chest,
they waited for another messenger,
        someone to write their names
        with a seagull's wing.

Why did they own this silence?
        What led them to this far place
where all the wrong animals lived?

Beneath the snow there were brambles
        and beneath the brambles clay,
        the hardest layer
they named for the English king.

Bareboned winters. Drenched hair.
Coins in the mouth of a fish.

All they wanted was a flawless green,
        a sky that smelled like rain,
something more sacred
        than a rabbit pelt nailed to a tree.

CHARLES FLOWERS
The Way We Were

The east village glows with slush in early February.
It's Monday & the week seems endless
at the Second Avenue Laundromat, where a girl
with cropped green hair & silver nose ring
sits reading *Portrait of a Lady*, while two waiters
from the Indian restaurant across the street
wash & fold a pile of burgundy tablecloths.
A trace of cardamom & cumin cuts
into the warm, soapy smell of love, which hangs
over all in this place, even the gym queen
who pouts while his boyfriend sorts their Calvins.
When the radio turns to all news,
the Latina laundress stops making change to reach
for the dial & a sad, clear voice fills the room,
which seems to sigh as the present slips away.
The girl with green hair stops reading
to stare at the dryer, thinking of the farm
in Wisconsin where her mother
hangs their sheets out to dry in the wind.
The waiters stop folding to smile
at one another, as if to croon like shiva divas,
while the pouty boy rises to tickle
his boyfriend, who's lipsynching, eyes closed,
remembering their first kiss.
And me with my *Voice*, projecting nostalgia
onto strangers, willing the present
back to a memory of wanting to be held
by my father, my desire unnamed,
before boys, before I glimpsed the way I would be.

What can heal the churning

shame of childhood? Only the future forgives,

the image of yourself

beyond the present, which allows you

to smile at strangers listening to Barbra,

whose voice carries me into the winter night,

whole & alone & humming.

JEFFREY THOMSON
Imaginary Numbers ⓒⓓ

$$i^2 = {}^-1$$

As in light coming distances
in the humming blankness
from stars already shuttered
and collapsed, as in the volume
of water not in a bottle, the area
of the shadow of a missing limb.
The way winter light through
glass warms nothing. The speed
at which, on the rain-slick
leaf-scattered Kittaning Pike,
the accident doesn't happen,
the car doesn't slew and swing
out against the oncoming traffic,
the horns don't blare, glass
doesn't turn to a geometry
of pain and so she returns home
after work with the dusk
already clambering up the house,
the porch light out, haphazard
mail and the message light
flashing down the hall.

It could be that her child,
gone to stay with his father,
has called to say he loves her,
or that her husband has left her
for another man, a rodeo clown,
and she won't know whether
to be enraged or amused.
Or perhaps it's her dentist
confirming her appointment
as her cats twine between
her legs, demanding to be fed.

If possibility is the square
of experience, what can she say

of this day, its unknown grief
haunting the house, painting
the walls with its brushwork
of headlight and shadow? Would
she wish to take it to the root,
the absolute *i* on the margins
of a tertiary world? Outside,
the rain begins again and
slaps the grass, the trees'
bare limbs scaffolding
the exponential dark.
She snaps on the light
and sees herself repeated
in the mirror, at once doubled
and inexplicably exhausted.

III

A SPLINTER BECOMING A BURNING PLANK
**Poems Disguised as Short Stories,
Condensed Novels, and Movie Treatments**

MICHAEL MCGRIFF
Coos Bay

The World's Largest Lumber Port,
the yellow hulk of Cats winding bayfront chip yards,
        caroling bargemen

looking for pussy, betting on high school football,
        abandoned Army barracks,
Japanese glass floats, cranberry bogs,

        mooring lines, salmon roe,
swing shifts, green chain, millwrights
        passing each other like black paper cranes

from one impermanence to the next,
        phosphorescent bay water, two tons
of oyster shells, seagulls, beach glass

        tumbled smooth in the surf, weigh stations,
off-bearing, front-loading, cargo nets,
        longshoremen, scabs,

the Indian casino marquee promising
        continental breakfast, star-crowned animals
stitched to blue heavens

        behind the fog, log booms,
choker setters, gypo outfits, acetylene sparks
        falling from the Coast Guard cutter *Citrus,*

dredging units, gravel quarries, clear cuts,
        scotchbroom taking over the dunes,
smokestacks pocked with peep shows

        of flame and soot, the year-round
nativity scene and one-armed Santa
        in J.C. Penney's alley window,

my grandmother dying just over the ridge,
        mother-of-pearl, sea lion calls
in the dark, low tide at Charleston Harbor,

        the sound of calk boots
in gravel parking lots, salmon sheen hosed
        onto the street, the arch

of a big rig's empty trailer, sand
        in all the moving parts,
floodlights, tie-downs, ridge beacons,

        great blue herons whispering through
the hollow reeds, Howard Cosell *Speaking of Sports*;
        the anecdotes of Paul Harvey, wishes of *good day*,

Patsy Cline going to pieces, my father's arm
        almost around me as we drive 101,
the cat-piss smell of a charred meth lab

        between the V.F.W. hall
and pioneer newspaper museum,
        the rusted scrapyard and tank-farm.

At the stoplight before the drawbridge
        we laugh at the women from the bank
falling out of their heels

        over the truck-grooved crosswalk—
the bridge spans forgotten coal bunkers,
        buried fingerprints of Chinese laborers,

rope-riders and mule bones.
        Back home we'll huddle around
the oil drum burn barrel,

a few weeks of newspapers
and wood scrap, trapped angels under the wire mesh
            my father and machinist neighbor

dying of cancer warm their hands over.
            The great heave of the Southern Pacific,
sturgeon like river cogs,

            barnacle wreckage, cattle-guards.
The last of the daylight,
            a broken trellis falling into the bay.

Michael McGriff on the subject matter of his poems
I tend to write poems about people from my hometown, which is a logging town on the southern Oregon coast, and you have to do a lot of self-interrogation when you're writing about a real life or a real situation. It's tricky when you take that as your subject. You can tend to make a melodramatic poem about a real situation by sidestepping the more difficult things to talk about. So I get a lot of pleasure when I write a poem and I feel like I've really been honest with the subject matter.

ADRIAN BLEVINS
Why the Marriage Failed ⓒ

After Gerald Stern

From the beginning it was the money, how we would not or could
  not make it.
It was never avarice, I resent the implication, it was how much like
  starlings
children are with those same raggedy screechings and us such
  languid nest makers:
him with his camera pointed up and me in the chair with the Plath
  in my lap.

From the beginning it was our innocence, it was our impertinence,
  it was a bent outhouse
in the dead dead double-dead clot of twisted winter. It was him
  with the black cloth
over his shoulders and that huge camera for a face and my face
  also like an infant's
in the photos he made. It was stupidity and I don't mind saying it,
  for we were farcical,

we were illogical, we were like a circle spinning and just that
  hollow—
we were the fragrance of the idea of the meaning of not. We didn't
  want destruction,
we were totally against *that,* so we made it our philosophy: we
  sought
a garden of Black-eyed Susans because all we wanted was to frolic

because like everyone else, we just wanted to be happy. But we
  were too wet,
we were like fog, we were an orchard of water in a cabin, stupor
  gone amuck.
We'd sit on the porch and look for some fields to farm, but we were
  too fertile
and didn't have hoes. We were minus a measuring cup and missing
  an umbrella

when you two boys got here and that was it, we were history. There were
maybe three candies in our pockets, but we weren't blank, we were stuffed
from loving you—we'd stare at your craving mini-mouths mid-shriek
and go *oh my god how entirely exquisite oh my god what have we done.*

Adrian Blevins with advice to young writers

Pay as particular attention as you can to the world because that is what all the best writing is made of. Look at it. Be a scientist of the world in order to make art of it.

EVIE SHOCKLEY

à table

aux ménétriers et robolins

they love him and i was with him:
        so they passed me the baguette,
to rip off a fist-sized chunk, golden

crust flaking onto the tablecloth
        in a crisp snow: they served up
salmon, smoked, with dill sauce,

thin slices of color itself: they
        tossed simple salads, lettuce
and oil, and stuffed tomatoes

for us, the vegetarian they love
        and the woman he loves: they
put out plates of cheese, insisted

i try a bit of *chevre* so strong it could
        have lifted the goat it came from:
they initiated me into the art

of the *apértif,* cassis, just so much,
        and chardonnay, electric currants
in a glass: they knew we could not

have food like this *aux états-unis,*
        melon as delightful as a silk
blouse against the shoulders, no,

wine as full and textured as sex,
        not possible, not to be believed
of the land of pagan cuisine: they

demanded, every uncle, aunt,
        and cousin, that we open our mouths,
throw back our heads, and swallow

all the family they could fit into one
            two-week visit: they hosted lunches
that lasted from noon to nine, dinners

that kept us feasting till we could
            neither sit nor stand: they produced
omelettes that rose above the pan's

edge like sunrise: they emptied
            their kitchens into our sated stomachs,
and when we were staggering under

a half-dozen courses, they presented
            the irresistibles, the *tartes* topped
with beautiful fruit, the chocolate

gateaux, the *flans,* and floating islands
            of meringue that some or all of us
must have dreamed up: they loved

us with rich, black coffee sweetened
            with honey from their hives: they
taught me their tongue: their toasts,

their jokes, their silences, their loud
            beliefs and quiet griefs, all the things
they bring to their tables: they taught me

how to be a part of them, who are a
            part of him, and i am replete with
kith and kin: i am gourmet, *gourmande.*

ILYA KAMINSKY

We Lived Happily During the War

and when they bombed other people's houses, we

protested
but not enough, we opposed them but not

enough. I was
in my bed, around my bed America

was falling: invisible house by invisible house by invisible house.

I took a chair outside and watched the sun
                                        in the sixth month
of a disastrous reign in the house of money

in the street of money in the city of money, in the country of money,
our great country of money, we (forgive us)

lived happily during the war.

Ilya Kaminsky on revision
The poems are never really finished of course, everybody would tell you that.
How do I know that they're not finished? Well, every time I read poems out
loud from a book, I find myself really wildly wanting to change line breaks,
and really wanting to read it a different way the next time I read it. And that's
how I know that the revision process continues even during the reading of
a specific poem.

SHERWIN BITSUI
Atlas

Tonight, I draw a raven's wing inside a circle
      measured a half second
            before it expands into a hand.
      I wrap its worn grip over our feet
            as we thrash against pine needles inside the
            earthen pot.

He sings an elegy for handcuffs,
      whispers its moment of silence
at the crunch of rush-hour traffic,
and speaks the dialect of a fork lift,
      lifting like cedar smoke over the mesas
            acred to the furthest block.

Two headlights flare from blue dusk,
      —the eyes of ravens peer at
Coyote biting his tail in the forklift,
      shaped like another reservation—
            another cancelled check.

One finger pointed at him,
that one—dishwasher,
he dies like this
      with emergency lights blinking through the creases of his
            ribbon shirt.

A light buzzed loud and snapped above the kitchen sink.
I didn't notice the sting of the warning:
      Coyote scattering headlights instead of stars;

howling dogs silenced by the thought of the moon;

constellations rattling from the atmosphere of the quivering gourd.

How many Indians have stepped onto train tracks,

      hearing the hoof beats of horses

      in the bend above the river

            rushing at them like a cluster of veins

scrawled into words on the unmade bed?

In the cave on the backside of a lie

      soldiers eye the birth of a new atlas,

one more mile, they say,

            one more mile.

ELIOT KHALIL WILSON
Last Day with Mayflower ⓒⅅ

We slept on ripped quilts in the trailer's shade
or on pads in the cab between jobs.

The boss called us *backs*—our animal use—
and I was a *back* in the grey Navy town.

We sweated in the long pants they made us wear
but few of the men I worked with cared—
most had just come from state prison or jail.

This was a two-truck, no-piano move—
all a young housewife's things, bound for storage.
Her husband, dead and buried at sea.

We saw him in the newspapers we used
to wrap china and all the fragile things.
Dress whites, white smile, an Annapolis degree—
a crisp officer on a submarine.

He died in sunlight, a calm dry-ground day,
his jeep, his last dumb moment, and a train.
Now the house they bought became a train to her.
Their togetherthings became a train.

II. That April I worked with Booze and Davis,
four-handed Booze our shoplifting king,
and Davis of sharpened screw-driver fame.
Davis was born tired and raised lazy.
They'd talk and laugh for ten hours a day.

I grew to like them—the way one can like
a man who lifts the other end of a dresser
or even takes the heavy end and walks backwards
down the stairs and up the ramp when you're sick
or too stoned or hung-over to lift much.

We were takers of sorts, a home turned house.
Making echoes by slow degrees
done when the house rang hollow and vast,
like the air inside a tire or a church.

III. The young widow was beautiful that day
in her heavy grief and her bravery
and she was kind to us though we walked in
like children who'd been kept from all sadness,
singing, even, and blasting the radio,
to try and drown the dull work in music.

She'd stand on the porch and stare at the truck
with great blue red-rimmed eyes and then she would
bring boxes of china and books to the ramp.
She brought us cold water and sandwiches.

The last to be moved was the barber's chair.
It sat in the den, an enameled anchor.
Her husband's chair from his father's will.

IV. She seemed to want to carry it alone.
She had tipped it on its side and pulled it,
all wrong, with her arms and it left a long
gash in the polished hardwood floor.
Next she hooked her fingers under the headrest
and pulled the weight against her chest
as one rows a boat or pulls a fishing net
until the blood in her arms and legs drained
and she dropped the chair heavily down.

How I wanted Booze and Davis to be quiet then.
I wanted not to have to ask them this.
Not to laugh at her in the hollow house.

This would be my last day, my first day, moving.

I should have said then—but how could I?—
that there must be a snow-quiet for her,
a slow quiet like the river tides,
the blue silence of a tired star,
the kind of silence that follows a train.

Eliot Khalil Wilson on poetic meter
I always pick blank verse or something like blank verse, ten-syllable lines, or
nine or eleven. It gets me just enough out of my voice so that it's interesting.

ANTHONY WALTON
Third Shift ⓒⓓ

Mickey says hey
you guys, go throw
eleven, which means
for me and Knox
to unstack
and stack a hundred
hundred pound sacks
of corn starch
or dextrose or whatever
off a truck out of
St. Louis or Decatur
or Kansas City.
Midnight, and we
will be loading
and unloading until
dawn. Next it might
be barrels of animal
fat bound for Memphis
or sifted grain destined
for the breakfasts
of the middle west.
We don't know
or care, we just
throw it, get out
of the way, and stand
on the dock taking deep
breaths and waving
the next guy in.
Then maybe it's
break, Knox and me
on the roof, him smoking
and singing about some
woman or another
and making bad jokes
about misery loving
company. I smile,
and because he knows
it will make me laugh

he sings "Since I Fell
For You" off-key
and with the wrong
words, and I look out
over the highway
toward Iowa wondering
which headlights
are headed here.
Then I take a hit
and it's time to go
back. It is always time
to go back. I am thinking
of a night when I was
younger and among the many
things I did not know
was that life could be
like this. I took Amtrak
out of South Bend
headed home to bury
a friend. In Chicago
the train stopped
behind a mill in Hegewisch
and I could see
a man sweating and stoking
a coke furnace.
It was late August, the sky
was going orange to pink
and it looked like he
was working the gates
of hell. I am learning
to think of these gates
as such, because it's hotter
than hell, Mickey is cursing
the day he was born,
Knox is singing about
misery, which is its own

company, and two more
trucks are backing in, steady
as the gravity dragging
us into the ground.

GIBSON FAY-LEBLANC
Oakland Work Crew

Dan said, My life is a nine with the hammer cocked,
chuckled, told of standing on a browned lawn
naked, three hundred pounds of pure Mick-Spic,
shooting at a Chevelle, tire marks on concrete.
Told how, *inside*, you heat a sharpened Bic
and a guy carves DannyBoy or Norteaño on your neck.

Prince talked of faint patterns on ceiling tiles
in his dreams and a pot with a ten in it when he finds
where color begins. He brought a picture: he's thirteen,
Liberia, wide smile, fatigues, kalishnikov
hugging his shoulder. Told of barefoot soccer,
running on bricks, the grace of a clean pass.

Rich said, I'm worth more than someone I meet,
then talked of his daughter, his girl, and ladies
here, there. He explained what it means to be
a baldhead, why, if he sees a Sudeaño on Third,
he can't be held responsible for what'll happen.
Told us which old school Cutlass' is hella tight.

Larry kept saying, High as an Oaktown sky,
and that's all he said, aside from seeing vines
or brush or poison oak we cut and pulled
as a J with a hit so big he'd vanish. Never
told us what we knew: clapboard house,
cracked talk, brothers to keep in shoes.

And I went home and wrote a lover, told
how far hills were no matter where I drove,
how I didn't know what it was to be a tatted
baldhead, raise kids, play barefoot in the street,
one eye on the hammer, one ear to the barrel,
hearing a seashell inside the chamber.

MAJOR JACKSON
Selling Out ⓒ

for Mat Johnson

Off from a double at McDonald's,
no autumnal piñata, no dying
leaves crumbling to bits of colored
paper on the sidewalks only yesterday,
just each breath bursting to explosive fog
in a dead-end alley near Fifth, where on
my knees, with my fingers laced on my head
and a square barrel prodding a temple,
I thought of me in the afterlife.
Moments ago, Chris Wilder and I
jogged down Girard, lost in the promise
of two girls who winked past pitched
lanes of burgers and square chips
of fish, at us, reigning over grills and vats.
Moments ago, a barrage of beepers
and timers smeared the lengths of our chests.
A swarm of hard-hatted dayworkers
coated in white dust, mothers on relief,
the minimum-waged poor from the fast-
food joints lining Broad, inched us closer
in a check-cashing line towards the window
of our dreams,—all of us anxious to enact
the power of our riches: me in the afterlife.
What did it matter, Chris and I still
in our polyester uniforms caked
with day-old batter, setting out
for an evening of passion marks?
We wore Gazelles, matching sheepskins,
and the ushanka, miles from Leningrad.
Chris said, *Let's cop some blow* despite
my schoolboy jitters. A loose spread
of dealers preserved corners. Then a kid,
large for the chrome Huffy he pedaled,
said he had the white stuff and led us
to an alley fronted by an iron gate on
a gentrified street edging Northern Liberties.
I turned to tell Chris how the night

air dissolved like soil, how jangling
keys made my neck itch, how maybe
this wasn't so good an idea, when
the cold opening of gun-barrel
steel poked my head, and Chris's eyes
widened like two water spills before
he bound away into a future of headphones
and release parties. Me? The afterlife?
Had I ever welcomed back the old
neighborhood? Might a longing
persistent as the seedcorn maggot
tunnel through me? All I know:
a single dog barked his own vapor,
an emptiness echoed through blasted
shells of rowhomes rising above,
and I heard deliverance in the bare
branches fingering a series of powerlines
in silhouette to the moon's hushed
excursion across the battered fields
of our lives, that endless night
of ricocheting fear and shame.
No one survives, no one unclasps
his few strands of gold chains
or hums "Amazing Grace" or pours
all his measly bills and coins into the trembling,
free hand of his brother and survives.
No one is forced facedown and waits
forty minutes to rise and begin again
his march, past the ice-crusted dirt,
without friendship or love, who barely knew
why the cry of the earth set him running,
even from the season's string of lights,
flashing its pathetic shot at cheer—to arrive
here, where the page is blank, an afterlife.

CURTIS BAUER

A Splinter Becoming a Burning Plank ⓒⁿ

If you run your hand down
the length of a 2" x 6" piece of age-smoothed pine
to feel the grain of the wood and you
don't lift it in time to keep the timber
from becoming part of your palm,
like you became part of the girl
everyone had kissed by the end of summer
in a ditch beside a gravel road,
the pain you feel isn't immediate
like the sky above you or the ground
humming between your feet. So
you might look at the four-inch splinter
piercing the flesh that used to be yours
and consider a word like *acumen*, or *sapience*;
you might think of the farmer who fell
from the hay loft onto a pitchfork
upturned in the manger
then walked to the house
to die in the arms of his wife,
but now the pain is rushing
your mouth and can't wait to squeeze
out, reckless like suffering built
up over time, and you wonder
if words like *love* and *death* have
anything to do with a splinter, with
a cracked piece of pine useless like
an image that has been folded too thin
over years to hold a memory of desire or duty
from wandering through
like the steers standing on the lawn
the morning the farmer walked out
of his house to feed them.

They stood as if the feedlot
had a welcome mat
and they'd wanted to wipe
their hooves before stepping back
into the rain-cleansed lot, but chance

left them dumb with new freedom
to track the green lawn a black
that would take months
of rain and heat to erase.
They were out because they could be,
because the posts and planks
that stretched to make a lot
had shattered in the herd's silent push
out of the barn, and
before they were aware of place
they stood outside the lot looking
in at the others looking out,

like the night twenty years before
when you sat in a ditch with a girl
and two other boys and waited your turn
for a kiss. The men at the party stood
at a cattle tank filled with beer and ice
and smoked and talked while the women
whispered at the picnic tables. Someone
shouted above the music, above the yellow
yard light creating a line of hidden and seen,
for more rocky mountain oysters,
more beer. Laughter rolled across
the lawn like soft wind through summer
tall weeds, and the cattle nudging through
the dark in the pasture beside the ditch and
the corn across the road standing
in its communal murmur watched it pass.

Each boy was having his turn.
Young enough to feel your heart
leap with each kiss, you were the inexperienced
son of a farmer who would one day hire
you out to her father. Was she responsible
for teaching you more than desire or
was her kindness the agonizing death
waiting on the tines of a pitchfork? If you say

she held your hand while she kissed your
brother and that changed your life forever,

say you have thought about that kiss
every night, and didn't know how to
remember it so maybe none of this
would have happened. Now
there should be silence and open space,
and dark because it's almost winter
and you have not seen any of these things.
You are in this poem because I don't have
the courage to say I've forgotten
it was me touching the lips of a girl
in the dark, feeling the stab of a splinter,
or that the man falling on the pitch fork
was really my grandfather who fell through
the floor of a corncrib and walked to his
house on a crushed ankle but didn't
want to die or be held by
the arms of the woman he didn't love.

Ninety-seven was the worst year, and I am back
at the barn where I watched my hand
become foreign. The wind stopped blowing
three months ago, after the night
it mowed the windbreak pine and dappled
the barn and house roof with holes.

The fallen trees are piled below
the cottonwood waiting for someone
to start the fire that will burn the sun-dried
leaves and pine needles, the twigs and branches
caked with sap that will catch and pull the flame
inside and bellow smoke out to lose itself in
the color of bleached sky.
This man sits while I stand; we watch
the fire grow and the air fill with ash
as old as the wind that carries it. The empty

sound of the barn and corncribs, the cattle lots
and farrowing house are disguised as wood
snapping and fighting the fire's heat, unwilling
to burn before its time—there is no use.
Like the splinter inside my palm,
like this man fallen through the floor, like
the boy after he'd acted like a man, the fire
catches and burns from the center out and
fills the air with sparks that catch the hog house
roof and a pile of planks this man remembers
lay in its rafters. Maybe he knew their worth
and mine, maybe he asked if I would save
the wood because he'd lived his life saving,
maybe there was disgust and despair
in his voice when he'd realized
I hadn't learned what he wanted.

If the wood was a man waiting to die,
and the flames licking the rafters a man
waiting to forget, nothing would change.
I refused. Fear is easy in the face of fire,
beneath the shingles trickling tar drops,
under the weakened rafters collapsing
and the planks popping and snapping
inside the shrinking walls, but salvation
is a trick to make us think.
We watched, my grandfather squinting
from his chair, me standing with my hands
in tact, wondering if anything turned out
the way it was planned. If I could say
the wrong fire was started by the wind
that splintered the trees, and the wrong boy kissed
the wrong girl, and the wrong man was dying
in the chair beside me I would pray
to the god of smoke and the god of stench
and the god of this man's thoughts
to become the wind and blow this fire
down to a lingering flicker that won't burn

the charred bark to cinders and scatter it
across the fields, but leave the fire-hollowed
trunks broken and black, oblivious
to the rain and wind and let them both
creep slowly back into the ground.

Curtis Bauer on revision

Revision is where life comes to the piece of writing; there's discovery there, elements in a poem can take shape in the third or fourth draft, that had I only tried writing it one time, that poem wouldn't have had the life, the integrity, the energy that it ends up having after numerous drafts.

ROSS GAY

How To Fall in Love With Your Father

Put your hands beneath his armpits, bend your knees,
wait for the clasp of his thinning arms; the best lock
cheek to cheek. Move slow. Do not, right now,

recall the shapes he traced yesterday
on your back, moments before being wheeled to surgery.
Do not pretend the anxious calligraphy of touch
was sign beyond some unspeakable animal stammer. Do not

go back further into the landscape of silence you both
tended, with body and breath, until it nearly obscured all
but the genetic gravity between you.

And do not imagine wind now blowing that landscape
into a river which spills into a sea. Because it doesn't.
That's not this love poem. In this love poem
the son trains himself on the task at hand,
which is simple, which is, finally, the only task
he has ever had, which is lifting
the father to his feet.

Ross Gay on his writing time

I write when I can. Anytime there's enough time to make it happen. Happens
that I drive a lot. Lately it seems that a lot of my writing gets done in the car.
So, I'll be driving from place to place and I'll be composing poems. When
there is free time, so called, I also write then. But, there is certainly no ritual.
I don't burn candles and I don't sacrifice animals. I just try to make sure I
have a pen and something to write on.

ROGER BONAIR-AGARD

called: Eurydice

a young black woman remembers 1870

1.

I do not come when called
Mostly I materialize

Dark as a kiss
incarnate again
    and again
sometimes twice in one life
now mother
    now the burnt sugar sweet
of a wide-eyed wide-hipped
too-young lover

now concubine
now priest

I do not come
I am called
when the wayward rib
needs me

2.

America is a dark continent
1878   exploding
industrializing
all over   my black behind

When I am called
I arrive   black bitch
whore   hard-ass
when I am called
    I run fugitive
slave-codes   Reconstruction
I've incarnated into the open
swinging

rotted mouths of my own lovers
just to know   like they know
burnt

3.
I dance in the clearing
I laugh too loud
I give benediction
I show off my knickers
    and smell like funk
    like ragtime
    like fiddle and bucket-bass
I walk the long road North
I come when called
I ghost
I materialize
I moan
I dark continent
            sweating
I incarnate
    then come

I high-lace collar
    pretending
I don't shuck and jive
I survive
I nigger   I black
I fuck massa in the barn
I serve tea in the big house
I collect Oscar and whipped back
I exposed super-bowl nipple
I Hottentot
I dark continent
don't tell me 'bout Africa
no more

Amos and Andy are coming
Toni Morrison is coming

Michael Jackson and Tito Puente are coming
Tuskegee and Kent State are coming
Muhammed Ali is coming
Clarence Thomas and Condoleeza
I incarnate I birth pain
I know the bird
of my next life
            singing
coming
    called
                    mother
    concubine
    songbird
            priest
fuck for love
for power
tomorrow
            I traitor   conscience
            fading
                    come

Roger Bonair-Agard on "called: Eurydice"

"called: Eurydice" is an ekphrastic poem, written from a photo from the late 1800s. My idea was to try to inhabit not just the body and voice but the spirit of the woman in the photo. I decided after a while of living with the picture, walking around with the picture in my bag, staring at it, that she was in effect, Eurydice, a multi-dimensional ghost, who in this case, being a black woman, was multi-dimensional in the way that one must be multi-dimensional in order to survive as a person of color. Once I had decided that about the character, it then became about, who are these different people she's inhabiting? Why is she inhabiting these different people? Where is she inhabiting them, and how many different times, and therefore, how many different movements?

TINA CHANG

Invention ⓒ

On an island, an open road
where an animal has been crushed
by something larger than itself.

It is mangled by four o'clock light, soul
sour-sweet, intestines flattened and raked
by the sun, eyes still savage.

This landscape of Taiwan looks like a body
black and blue. On its coastline mussels have cracked
their faces on rocks, clouds collapse

onto tiny houses. And just now a monsoon has begun.
It reminds me of a story my father told me:
He once made the earth not in seven days

but in one. His steely joints wielded lava and water
and mercy in great ionic perfection.
He began the world, hammering the length

of trees, trees like a war of families,
trees which fumbled for grand gesture.
The world began in an explosion of fever and rain.

He said, Your body came out floating.
I was born in the middle of monsoon season,
palm trees tearing the tin roofs.

Now as I wander to the center of the island
no one will speak to me. My dialect left somewhere
in his pocket, in a nursery book,

a language of childsplay. Everything unfurls
in pictures: soil is washed from the soles of feet,
a woman runs toward her weeping son,

chicken bones float in a pot full
of dirty water. I return to the animal
on the road. When I stoop to look at it

smells of trash, rotting vegetation,
the pitiful tongue, claws curled tight
to its heart; eyes open eyes open.

When the world began in the small factory
of my father's imagination he never spoke
of this gnarled concoction of bone and blood

that is nothing like wonder but just the opposite,
something simply ravaged. He would die soon after
the making of the world. I would go on waking,

sexing, mimicking enemies. I would go on coaxed
by gravity and hard science while he rested in the satin
of his shriveled skin. Eyes swollen to exquisite planets.

SARAH MESSER

I am the Real Jesse James

It took four men with big heavy hands to hold the horse down. The horse kicked its stomach, collapsed like an ironing board and rolled over, pinning the legs of the men beneath it. One man sat on its neck while the other administered the needle—Bute and Demerol in the night paddock. The horse's eyes were like stoplights in the head-lights of the men's trucks parked in a circle around the animal. I have faced this animal in a paddock when it was too late to run. I was young but I was no girl when my hand came down hard on the muz-zle of the horse that charged, half a ton of meat and muscle thrown my way.

*

I am the real Jesse James. I have stared down that stampede, that rage he thinks belongs only to him. I heard it took four men to hold him down when his mouth frothed and he swore and spit and bit people, had to be held down against the smashed furniture. This rumor follows him like a legend, like a bad smell. An animal that can be held down by four grown men. But what kind of animal is that? A horse that kicks its own stomach. A thought that eats away at men's guts when they are already trapped, already tamed. The one last thing that she should have told him but didn't; the one time he reached for her and she turned away. I am the real Jesse James. Not the man you may have heard of held down by four men, his friends who ran after him when he drank too much as usual and was off like a horse out of the bar and down the street and into the forest of buildings, the forest of his own thoughts, all the things he should have told her.

*

Perhaps you have heard about my legend? The one that follows me like a hang-over, a bad smell. It was rage that held the big animal down in the paddock, not the heavy hands of the men who pinned it there in the dirt that wasn't a paddock really, just the circle of their trucks parked and running. This happened when I was just a girl, so it is hard to remember. I watched as it took two of them to hold the neck down and administer the needle—Bute and Demerol. One man sat on the horse's neck and said: this is one sick horse, fucking bastard. The men were angry, standing in front of their trucks after chasing the horse across the field, through a forest of trees and I wasn't supposed to follow.

*

I am the real Jesse James. I know you have heard of me. That was what I was supposed to say, the last thought before I turned my head away from him and he flew into a rage. I am the real Jesse James. But I have drunk far too much tonight. And I am just a girl. Perhaps you have heard of his legend? It took four men to hold him down in the paddock after he ran out of the bar, four of his friends to hold him down because rumor has it that he smashed some furniture. I have seen this man naked and I can tell you that he is no Jesse James. I am the real thing. I mean, I am telling you the real story now. But I have drunk far too much tonight. And I am just a girl.

*

What is known about the doctor who helped the outlaw Jesse James when he was wounded, rolling in a frothy rage and held down by four men in a paddock: He brought his doctor's bag with him. Needles, Bute, Demerol. The doctor did not know he was helping an outlaw. When he entered the circle of trucks the men had parked with the engines running, the air smelled like horses let loose from barns. The outlaw Jesse James was a small girl held down by four men. She was in a rage—having smashed furniture and split a man's lip, kicked him in the stomach. Why had the men been holding her down, the doctor asked, couldn't they see she was just a girl? The air smelled like outlaws and the girl said, I am the real Jesse James, you aren't gonna tell on me, are ya, doc?

*

The doctor lived in a red house that burned light from the inside. When he walked out the red door, the air smelled like a legend. Somewhere out in a field, four men were holding a girl down by the legs, they were kneeling on her neck. Her eyes were stop lights in the air that smelled like the men's breath, like the inside of whiskey glasses. They said they were looking for a friend who ran away and they talked about him as if he were some sort of outlaw, as if he were the real Jesse James.

*

The horse, the girl said, the horse has escaped its stall, is running out in the night, has broken out of the barn. I am no girl. And I am no doctor, the doctor thought, I am a thief. I steal from medicine cabinets. The girl rides the horse to all her private robberies. Who has stolen her horse? The doctor placed a hand on the girl's neck where the boot had been. He felt a vein pulse. A red house that burned light from the inside. Isn't it always rage, the doctor thought, that makes one body hold another to the ground like some sort of legend? The men are all outlaws. They are all little girls who need to be held down and given medicine. She needed this medicine, the men told the doctor. Her mouth was a red house that burned light from the inside. I am no girl, she said, I am the real Jesse James. The men drank too much tonight and could not find their friend. The doctor placed his bag down in a circle of dirt, in the air that smelled like whiskey. I am no doctor, he said.

*

When I was a girl, my father was a doctor who lived in a house that caught fire and burned red from the inside. He was always falling asleep with a needle in his arm, burning things down. He was always running away from his four friends, those men with heavy hands who used to chase him out of bars and down the street through a forest of buildings, his own thoughts that were filled with the smell of burned houses, horses and the outlaw Jesse James. That night I watched the men driving their trucks across the fields. The trucks stopped with their headlights in a circle, the engines running. I was riding my horse through the forest until he sweated with rage, his mouth foaming, his red coat burning from the inside against my legs. I was just a girl and I was not supposed to follow the men when they drove their trucks across the field looking for my father with his doctor's bag caught in the circle of light, his eyes burning red stop lights when he said where is my girl? And the men's hands were on him.

*

But the men, were not outlaws. They held themselves down with their own hands. The doctor came with his bag and gave them clean needles. The air carried the smell of horse on its back. The men talked to each other as if they were creating a legend. Each of them said I am the outlaw, I am the real thing, the one who ran out of the bar and into the streets and give me your hands, go ahead put your hands on me and try to hold me down now that my veins burn red from the inside. I am a horse that rolls over on your legs and pins you down. And what do you think I am? Do you think I am a girl? I am no girl. Did I tell you that before I left she let four men put their hands on her? She let them hold her down to the ground.

*

There was a girl I loved who was a legend among her friends. They said that she was prone to fly into rages and sometimes just ran out of bars and into the streets. I was no doctor, but I could tell this girl needed help. Rumor had it she smashed some furniture, burned letters, and split the lip of her friend, all because a man turned himself away from her at the wrong time. I loved her, yes, but there is no point in making a legend of it. Jesse James was shot by a friend in his own home. But in his photo, they crossed his hands over his chest in a restful pose.

Sarah Messer on how poems look on the page
Sometimes I do employ an external structure on the poem, like on the Jesse James poem; the poem had to fit a half-folded page, typed, and also, I think a formal constraint was that I had to use a typewriter—a manual typewriter-—which makes you sort of write differently.

IV

LATE TWENTIETH CENTURY IN THE FORM OF LITANY
Poems that Use Repetition Very Very Well

CHRISTIAN BARTER
The Phoenix

Being ash, being dust,
being what's left on the plate,
being the bungalow with a moss-eaten roof
a stone's throw off from the new glass house,

being bone and gristle,
being biomass,
being something stuck to the fridge floor
whiffing of a long-turned tide,
being shredded, un-sought secrets,
being car exhaust,
being half-buried rusted-out bedsprings
sleeping it off in the woods,

being what was washed from the photo by the years,
being what will never wash,
being what's in the storm drain hurrying off,

the dust flaring up in the comet's tail,
the toe-nail clippings feeling around under the rug,
the sticks laid out on the highway after a storm,
the pennies on the dashboard short of a dollar,
the hollow core of an old swamp cedar,
the crumpled butt of the sweetest cigarette
you ever had, I am

everywhere and I demand my wings.

Christian Barter on getting to the good stuff
When I sit down with a strategy in mind, it's often because I've read something that I really admire and I want to try to mine a little bit of the good stuff
that that poet's been able to mine. So I reach for the same tool, and start
picking away to see how's this thing going to work. Is it sharp enough, does
it get the good stuff out?

CURTIS BAUER

I'll Say It This Way

You are my 5th Avenue
You are my 6th my 8th my Broadway
You are my grain of salt my steak
  boiled baked and fried potatoes
  my sweet corn on the cob
You are my border crossing
You are my trans-Atlantic flight
  the long layover between London and Bilbao
You are my new pair of shoes
  the blisters they give my feet
  the sliced tomato in the fridge
  the smell in the sheets
  memory of your underwear drawer
  the cool in my drink
  humidity
You are the obituary on page A 17
  the sliver of photograph falling
  out of the folded-up letter I still
  haven't sent
You are radio static
You are the dream I had last night
  the night before
  I want tonight
You are the words
  I wish I'd written
You are anticipation
  the mistakes I've made
  the worst decisions I've made
  the moment I want to quit
You are the voice that says quit
You are the one for me
You two thousand miles away
You different languages spoken
You asleep right now while I write

KAZIM ALI

After I Said It

And after I said it
After I fell from the window

After I turned down the bed of history
Turned down the ocean road

Far enough down the ocean road
To dune-grasses, seagulls

In these other days
In another life

I did not say it
And in a different life

In my third life
I did not even think it

At the window
In my favorite blue shirt

Light sparkling up from the water
In my fourth life, angels

In my fifth life, windows

Kazim Ali on listening
I just think you have to have guts and to listen to the silence, and see what
you hear.

JOHN POCH

Jorie Graham

No one likes to lie or be lied to.
      —Jorie Graham

Once, I pressed my ear
against a doorframe in Iowa.
Picture a lover fresh from his beloved
trying hard to become a doorframe
through which that beloved will walk
and even sleepwalk. Listen.
Ants were eating the house,
and you could hear their fun.
The workers were so drunk with crunching
they would stagger out
from the baseboard like total tourists.
And I, a skyscraper.
The queen lay safe a hundred yards away,
which seemed a mile, while poem
after poem dropped from her body.
These were carried away
before she could mature them.
I am not obsessed with the queen.
I am not obsessed with the queen.
I am not obsessed with the queen.
She made me write this a hundred times
on the board after class one year.
The workers made fun and crunched.
The queen said, This boy is a liar;
now laugh at him. I stood
accused of imitating a doorframe,
of writing a sonnet.
I wish this were a sonnet.
I wish everything were one.
I stood there with my ear
like a flag on a pole
contemplating hospitality or revenge.
I chose nectar—that which overcomes death—
and I poured it on.

GILLIAN KILEY

The Barrel is Surely Coming Down the Hill

It would be good to brush the crumbs
from our shirtfronts. It would be good to walk
farther on, beyond the diagrammed neighborhoods
inscribed between highways, to pick up our feet with a purpose
other than to examine the pattern of tread.
Very specialized products are on the march,
outmoding once-blessed enterprises.
The old things have been pressed
into flat cakes for quick storage. My muffin
is on steroids and the defenses are not holding up,
and there are agonal mounds of sheddings, trash and dirt
painted over and cast as novelties or ignored,
and in the world of configurations of just-is, the real project
has been to deregulate the bonds
between events and the memory of events
so we can contain ourselves in the dark.
But when the light comes on all over town
it looks like a sudden failure of horses everywhere.

Gillian Kiley on reading her poems aloud when she writes
It helps me identify what needs to be cut out of a poem—whether my writing is too prosy, too silly, or too *something*. And it also helps me answer
questions about structure, so I can discover how long lines should be, or
where pauses should be, and if the pauses I have, or the stanza breaks I
have, are appropriate.

KEVIN GOODAN
to crave what the light does crave

to crave what the light does crave
to shelter, to flee
to gain desire of every splayed leaf
to calm cattle, to heat the mare
to coax dead flies back from slumber
to turn the gaze of each opened bud
to ripe the fruit to rot the fruit
and drive down under the earth
to lord a gentle dust
to lend a glancing grace to llamas
to gather dampness from fields
and divide birds
and divide the ewes from slaughter
and raise the corn and bend the wheat
and drive tractors to ruin
burnish the fox, brother the hawk
shed the snake, bloom the weed
and drive all wind diurnal
to blanch the fire and clot the cloud
to husk, to harvest,
sheave and chaff
to choose the bird
and voice the bird
to sing us, veery, into darkness

Kevin Goodan on the form a poem will take
A poem sort of arises organically as I'm typing it on the page. I do pay attention to various technical aspects of the poem, but I allow it to form itself on
the page. Sometimes, I do go back and make revisions and realize that
maybe the poem wants to be in couplets or maybe the poem wants to take
on the form of a sonnet. But, initially, that's not the case. I just let the poem
come out, and then through various stages of revision, I go back and tend
to its shape just a little bit.

ROGER BONAIR-AGARD

what the water gave me

after Frida Kahlo

The water gave me madness
incessant humming blood

the water remembers the torn torso
melting through a seashell's portholes

the quadrangular tight-rope of death
disease slaughtered women the trade
in gold and spirit of five hundred nations drifting

the water remembers   the water is clarity
the water remembers   offers back hurricane
the water remembers   hides its secrets

no wonder water remembers in tectonic shifts
and the angry expectorant of lava

no wonder water runs muddy revolts
to flood and brackish

no wonder water stays still in the dark
the water is coming back home

Roger Bonair-Agard on the form a poem will take
Even if I start to write a sestina, at some point I have to make the decision
whether or not the poem wants to be a sestina; whether or not what the
poem wants to say is actually going to be best supported by the sestina
form or by something else. And if it's something else, then I have to change
it. I hope I am getting better at being able to listen to what the poem wants
rather than to what my intention might have been going in.

SUZANNE CLEARY
Echocardiogram

How does, how does, how does it work
so, little valve stretching messily open, as wide as possible,
all directions at once, sucking air, sucking blood, sucking
    air-in-blood,
how? On the screen I see the part of me that always loves my life,
    never tires
of what it takes, this in-and-out, this open-and-shut in the dark
    chest of me,
tireless, without muscle or bone, all flex and flux and blind
will, little mouth widening, opening and opening and, then,
    snapping
shut, shuddering anemone entirely of darkness, sea creature
of the spangled and sparkling sea, down, down where light cannot
    reach.
When the technician stoops, flips a switch, the most unpopular kid
    in the class
stands off-stage with a metal sheet, shaking it while Lear raves.
So this is the house where love lives, a tin shed in a windstorm,
tin shed at the sea's edge, the land's edge, waters wild and steady,
    wild and steady, wild.

Suzanne Cleary on her writing process
When I begin writing a poem, I say to myself, "I don't know which words are
the poem itself, and which words are just the notes for the poem." This has
become a sort of mantra that reminds me to suspend judgment and just
write. I've learned that only later in the writing process should I distinguish
between good lines and bad, about winnowing the poem from the dross. It
allows me to write badly, even encourages me to write badly, which is to
say, boldly. Thus, it invites me into the arena where the best poems can happen, given time, faith, hard work, and luck.

SARAH MANGUSO
This Might Be Real

How long in a cold room will the tea stay hot?
What about reality interests you?
How long can you live?
Were you there when I said *this might be real?*
How much do you love?
Sixty percent?
Things that are gone?
Do you love what's real?
Is *real* a partial form?
Is it a nascent form?
What is it before it's real?
Is it a switch that moves and then is ever still?
Is it a spectrum of cross-fades?
Is what's next *real?*
When it comes will everything turn real?
If I drink enough tea to hallucinate, is that real?
If I know I'm waiting for someone but I don't know who, is he real?
Is he real when he comes?
Is he real when he's gone?
Is consequence what's real?
Is consequence all that's real?
What brings consequence?
Is *it* what's real?
Is *it* what turned everything to disbelief, the last form love takes?

Sarah Manguso with advice for young writers
Practice being a voice—to inhabit a voice other than yours and your understanding of your immediate experience. The pieces that arise from the technique of voice, those are poems.

ILYA KAMINSKY
Second Ending of the Fairy-Tale

Such is the story made of stubbornness and a little air,
a story sung by those who danced before the Lord in silence,
who whirled and leapt. Giving voice to consonants that rise
with no protection but each other's ears
we are on our bellies in this silence, Lord.

Let us wash our faces in the wind and forget the strict shapes of
    affection.
Let the pregnant woman hold something of clay in her hand
for the secret of patience (no secret) is more patience.
Let her man kneel on the roof, clearing his throat,
he who loved roofs, tonight and tonight, making love to her and
    her forgetting,
a man with a fast heartbeat, a woman dancing with a broom, uneven
    breath.
Let them borrow the light from the blind.
Let them kiss your forehead, approached from every angle.
What is silence? Something of the sky in us.
There will be evidence, there will be evidence.
Let them speak of air and its necessities. Whatever they will open,
    will open.

Ilya Kaminsky on the pleasure and pain of writing
Writing is not a therapy, it's an art. Anybody who tells you that you should sit
down and write your pain and that's it is telling you bullshit. Writing is an art
and it has to be well built. But, then, some years ago, a friend of mine who is
a wonderful poet told me just that sentence: writing is not a therapy, it's an
art. And I doubted that for a second. I thought, Hey, but your poems are very
therapeutic for me; they help me in my difficult moments. That's one thing
that I find great poetry does for me, that's the pleasure for me in reading. I
suppose that's also the pleasure in writing; it helps me to find out how to live.
But, I wouldn't advise it to anybody. You find yourself grasping, and trying,
and struggling to say something fairly obvious in three words, or three-and-
a-half words. And, words are not enough. And you continue beating your
head against the wall, and the wall doesn't break—your head does.

RUTH ELLEN KOCHER
gigan: xi. ⓒ

listen to the flock of grackles praising the just softening
fig, the disturbed hush brushed back by their wings,

the placid spiral of their hovered beaks bleating out
a black gravity, say the tree, say the fig's altar,
say the mute sugar invoking its seed, dark skin

purpled from green, say a woman whose eyes
close against their clawed and feathered descent,

a brutal harvesting, a hewn heart, the frictive
branches craggy in their upward reach. say here

is a bird, an animal that receives a feathered happening,
listens to the flocked emergence in its throat, imagined

by a woman whose brown eyes bloom inward
like the fig's implosive ripening or
assumption billowed in a velvet robe.

here is her mouth that opens like a fig.
listen to its plum valediction confess to be yours.

Ruth Ellen Kocher on the form of her "gigan" poems
I was trying to find a way to enter a poem that was not as convoluted and
muddled as my previous project. So, I developed this 16-line form that I call
a gigan, after my favorite Godzilla movie monster. The gigan is seven stanzas, a couplet, a triplet, couplet, couplet, couplet, triplet, couplet, with the
first line repeating as line 11, the sixth line repeating as line 12, and the last
couplet of the poem is a volta, or turn slightly away from the subject. As
convoluted as that sounds, it's been a very freeing exercise. Because the
form is predetermined, I've been able to divert my attention away from that
architecture and really concentrate on language.

MICHAEL MCGRIFF

Lines Written Before the Day Shift

Let me be the architect
in the glass city of your mouth.
The wild clock of your mouth
spins backwards: glass to sand,
sand to freshwater pearl.
Let me be the beekeeper, feather
merchant, knife-thrower, soothsayer,
the savant of your mouth.
The farrier with tested theories
of wear and distance,
the shoeing of your mouth,
the alchemy of it, its horse-drawn wheel.
Let me hoist half a sugared lemon
to the slick roof.

Because the mouth moves us
from one unknowing to the next,
let me banish the charted course,
theory, and fine angles;
let no mechanical lily
take root in its soil;
let nothing be raised
to its palate—no pale words,
no anvil's lust for iron, nor the hands of men.
Let nothing obscure the mystery
of the thumb-deep vault
of the thimbleberry of your open mouth
as you sleep under the dawn-flicker
of tea lights.

Let there be room enough
for the Weaver Maiden and Ox Driver
who lie shackled to polar banks
of the River of Heaven, where once a year
they cross those star-laced waters in your mouth
on a bridge of sparrows,
meet midway and lose themselves
wholly in each other like branches of wisteria.

Give me this star-tortured patience,
the yearning, this one night lived
and relived in the heavenly bodies
moving over the wings of your mouth.
One thimbleful of wet light
poured into another.

SARAH MESSER

America, the Hallelujah

According to thy word. Affliction is
a stormy deep. Again the day returns.
And there is, _____, a rest. Angels roll
the rock. Another day is past. Another
six days work. Another year. As the heart
with eager. Behold a stranger.
Brightest and best of bright. Brother,
thou art gone. Call me away. Flung
to the heedless. Forgive my folly.
From earliest dawn. From every
stormy. From Greenland's icy. Gently
glides the stream. Gently, O gently. Give
Glorious things. Had not a word. Happy
is he who. Happy the man whose. Hark!
what mean these. Hear what
the voice. How beautiful the sight. How
blest is every. How blest the man. How did
my heart. How precious is the—
                    I love the volume.
I'm but a stranger. I'm but a weary. I sing
the mighty. It's good to give. I waited meekly.
I would not live. Just as I am—
                    Let every creature.
Let us with joyful. Long as I live. My country
'tis of thee. My God, how endless. My never-
ceasing song. Nearer my God to thee. Now let me
make. O, come loud anthems. O, I could find.
O, for a shout. O, for a thousand. O happy
day that. O happy they who. See what a living.
Sing Hallelujah. So fades the lovely. Soft
be the gently. Softly they rest. So let our lips.

                    Soon as I heard.
The billows swell. The cloud hath filled.
The day is past. There is a land, a. There is
a land of. There is an hour. There is a stream.
There is a world. The voice of the free. The winter
is over. This is the word.

Tho' dark and stormy.
Through all the changing. Up to the fields.
We come with joyful. Welcome, delightful.
We sing the bright. When down our heads.
When I can read. When I can trust. When our
hearts are. When overwhelmed. Where shall the man.
Why is my heart. Ye boundless realms. Ye nations
of the.
Yes, my native land.
Ye sons of men, a. Ye sons of men, with.
Yes, there are joys. Yes, we trust the day.
Ye trembling captives.

Sarah Messer on America the Hallelujah
It's a "found poem," and I maintained the alphabetical order.

GABRIELLE CALVOCORESSI

Late Twentieth Century in the Form of Litany ⓒⅅ

after Tom Andrews

The winter continued and I thought I heard voices.
Butchers sharpened their knives and I thought I heard voices.
Roy Orbison moaned and I thought I heard voices.

In the dark room of childhood I thought I heard voices.
My bike chain came loose and I thought I heard voices.
Mother choked on the bit and I thought I hear voices.

A war raged outside and I thought I heard voices.
My saxophone gleamed and I thought I heard voices.
The drive-in went dark and I thought I heard voices.

The speakers kept sizzling and I thought I heard voices.
Boys came in the pews and I thought I heard voices.
Mother choked on the bit and I thought I heard voices.

The mills locked their doors and I thought I heard voices.
Elvis kept playing dead and I thought I heard voices.
I watched her undress and I thought I heard voices.

Boys lit cats on fire and I thought I heard voices.
Flames crept toward our yard and I thought I heard voices.
The Klan marched through town and I thought I heard voices.

I met my maker and I thought I heard voices.
Gas filled the garage and I thought I heard voices.
I lied at 's and said I heard voices.

Someone shot J.R. and I thought I heard voices.
She said, "Get me out" and I thought I heard voices.
My vision got worse and I thought I heard voices.

I crawled into bed and I thought I heard voices.
The highway came through and I thought I heard voices.
I met my maker and I thought I heard voices.

I danced in my bedroom and I thought I heard voices.
The curtains caught fire and I thought I heard voices.
Mother took all the pills and I looked at the clock.

I placed my hand on the turntable and I thought I hear voices.
Joan Jett sang *Crimson and Clover* and I thought I heard voices:
Over and over and I thought I heard voices.

BRIAN TURNER
The Hurt Locker

Nothing but the hurt left here.
Nothing but bullets and pain
and the bled out slumping
and all the *fucks* and *goddamns*
and *Jesus Christs* of the wounded.
Nothing left here but the hurt.

Believe it when you see it.
Believe it when a 12-year-old
rolls a grenade into the room.
Or when a sniper punches a hole
deep into someone's skull.
Believe it when four men
step from a taxicab in Mosul
to shower the street in brass
and fire. Open the hurt locker
and see what there is of knives
and teeth. Open the hurt locker and learn
how rough men come hunting for souls.

ROSS GAY

Cousin Drowses on the Flight to Kuwait ⓒⒹ

Do you dream of Saturn of molars
of the jeweled corridors of palaces dream
the commander's robes
his crooked smile dream
sooty bellows of cumulous
dream dress dream a lover's breath dream
wind over dunes the voices
riding night winds dream whispered
light of stars dream teddy bear dream mother
father dream baby
sister dream mirages
dream your body riding the air
dream the body's tenuous earthen cleave dream
birthmark or crooked toe
dream every hair on your head dream
galaxies aswirl at each finger's tip
the trigger's smooth tick
dream brown faces your
brown face dream the commander
cockeyed the tumble of diamonds stumbling
from his toothless mouth
his florid robes flailing above a fat body
dream the dragon's toothpick
fibula femur dream orchard abloom
in bloody soil dream
the improbability of your legs
ambulatory pleasures
sand frosty towpath gravel
road dream breezes combing
clover growth threading a graveyard's grass
dream the random calculus of shrapnel
or your skin wrapping the chorale of muscle
and bone the galactic swell
of blood cells heaving
breathe dream
breathe

V

SPANGLING THE SEA
Poems with Convincing Consonance and
Chimes of Internal Rhyme

JOHN POCH
Song

Now, there is a fine vine fire blue
green illusion in your arms
no couturier could deal,
no dress on a door could adorn,
a deliberate witchery of rhythm
in your sobbing. I want to be you,
and your cheek against my chest.
I am.
          I mean, yesterday
I was something else insignificant
like a chipped stack of black dishes.
Let some yard sale be done with them,
or send them to a tornadoed town.
Arrange them at the foot of a broken oak
with napkins and faux-fruit.

Are you one of the gods, girl?
With your prehensile style of loving,
you are the reason for groves.
There is no child in you, yet.
Let me say I will clothe the prairie
with a tablecloth of praise.
Bring nothing. Bring nothing.

ANTHONY DEATON
All Effect

For this reason hail in June
and how we read the season

jeremiad or excuse
to shelter in the park gazebo

as white granular ciphers
written hectic and sky-bitten

over the well-mannered lawn
spell birdsong despite it all

or because of it perhaps
grackles crowd lower boughs

keen and scold the wintry
missiles with shrill flushing

whistles that overbrim
loosening like unpent steam

from the tea kettle's grip
singing for this reason

your loose shoulder strap
a little falls a little falls

what your freckled shoulder means
on the tip of my tongue.

SEAN SINGER

Living On Nothing But Honey And Smoke (CD)

for Albert Ayler (1936–70) & Cleveland

Evergreen leather winterwear and a honky-tonk, but salty glissando,
a man revealing his baby-life in the dark, when the dark was a
scattered ambrosia,

but opening plaints with dynamite, and a grill and a tremolo and
hard plastic reed.
What is self-evident, he said, was a colored disk, a sword, the cup
of indignation.

*I have seen the bright wall of the universe, magnified ten times, and
eat only green*
things. But when President Johnson was a spooky longhorn, the
Pope got the message,

a clicking sound with his tongue, the spirit's balafon hymnic, the
freak bearing.
As the saxophone wends and balloons, so the vision. It wasn't
funny anymore.

Flowering in the very field, his legit sneers, he has sucked the air
out of the room,
mesmerized hyena, and brought us back on a kind of ship, afloat &
afflatus driftwood . . .

and the East River took us to the foot of Congress Street Pier where
our lungs had dried.
Become Ashtabula, taxonomic, a burned running, a fur peeling, a
pure feeling, an orange.

Become an admirer.

Become Olmstead, Parma, and Ashtabula, where translucent quays
burn with fox-oil,
overweight drivers, gray mosquitoes, a wood flushed with the
lashing waves of pine.

Her brunette radar zoned me, gathering buckeye, rucksack, and
   eyeglass cloth
we became river: Ashtabula was the orange wreck of bricks,
   boards, a nurse.

The mud slung me, part of the forest, to a new river. This isn't
   tenderness, you know:—
it's *worn*. The river, Little Cricket Neck, was burning mineral, iron
   filing, flies, and tires.

A marvel how rectangular fires make unearned past efforts, so we
   blazed, filthy nuggets,
to the utter gully, wherewith sky like Gethsemane, we sneaked into
   the guestroom, all cushiony.

At any rate, we were pierced. The clumps of soot hit the windows,
   all black now, & I exhaled.
Become a wizard, a ghost, a spirit, a saint, a bell, a Cleveland, the
   final cadence, two octaves up.

Become an admirer.

Become Ashtabula or become assiento, the darkness of river,
   aspergillic breaking into ashunch.
Become, yes, admirer.

Sean Singer on employing poetic form
The subject matter or the content of the poem will dictate what form the
poem will take. Emerson had this view that poems exist in some kind of pla-
tonic ether, and you just have to sort of figure out what the right words are
to pluck them out of the atmosphere, but I believe that a poem can't just be
any form, it has to be particular to what you're talking about and why you're
talking about it.

KEVIN GOODAN

The first sturdy bee begins

The first sturdy bee begins
To cross-pollinate the few flowers
Opened around the house.
It is March seventy degrees.
Last week saw snow on the ground.
A mosquito siphons my arm
And I do not smash it, stunned
As we are by being here.
Four lambs were born
And one is in the recycling bin
Dying. The ivy didn't
Survive the last hard cold spell.
Some things believed to be hardy
Are not so. I miss you.
Ewes remaining in birthing pens
Chomp grain and choice-cut, waiting.
Blackbirds in the hemlock vie
For respite. Slurry-bins
Steam, fragrant, field-side.
If there is danger, if no world lasts
Who's to say we were even here at all?

Kevin Goodan on reading his poems aloud when he writes
I tend to think of poetry, still, as an oral tradition and a literary tradition. So, when I write a poem, I'm often repeating the words out loud to myself to see if there are ways it could be heard differently or said differently. It's probably why I live alone, because I'd probably drive somebody absolutely bonkers if they had to listen to me do this all the time.

RODGER LEGRAND
Tar the Roof

Dirt blood, tar blood, mud
brain and eyes, trailer park
skull, trailers parked
on loose stones, exposed
to the cold, to those
who crawl under to hide
from the police, to stay out
of the cold, with their gold
teeth and needles. Tar the roof
in the summer, tar the aluminum
to keep leaks away
in winter. Tar streaks down
the sides, over windows, widows.
Seal the cracks, seal in the slaps,
the knickknacks, the front porch
booze attacks, weeds growing
through cracks in the sidewalk.
Ex-cons under trailers, ex-cons, pre-
cons, latch-key maybes, babies
in the street on big wheels,
trash heaps at the curb,
social services moving in
next door to not move in next door.
Beer bottles smashed across
the yard, smashed husbands
beating smashed wives.
Sex-ring next door, plywood
door, sky door, sky attic, cloud leaps,
sleep disturbed, scream heaps,
baby screams, lady screams, tires
screech, reach their peek with drug deals,
Meals On Wheels, time steals
from us, steal ourselves, steal
at backyard barbeque banquets,
yard sales, no sales, no time, no thoughts
but the roof, tar roof, tar brain, tar
windows and eyes, tar it in,
tar it in, tar the sky.

JAMES HOCH
The Court of Forgetting (CD)

The awkward-gaited, the under-ripe
jacked-up over-jerseyed teenage boys
spill onto the court, a slab of desert
beaten in the yard of this way-station
at the edge of the Reservation. The air-guitar
player, the air-baller, half-court rim-clanger,
the pimple-plagued conjurer of nipples,
the bible-thumping believer that lingerie
carries the meadow-scent of angels,
they're talking trash, snatching loose balls,
laying them softly off the plywood.
The one who lobs piss from the overpass,
one who siphons gasoline, huffs hours
crumpled in wood sheds, in warm oblivion,
they're perfecting crotch grab and spit,
and got a mean pick and roll going on.
The one who pries his mother's fingers
from beer cans, one who wires pickups
and ditches them in canyons, one who
swaggers and stares stone-inducing stares
before crossing over and driving to the hole,
they have the sweet, easy hands, and pray,
if only briefly, for the clean, wet sound
of ball swishing net. The one who has taken
his uncle's prick in his mouth, the one
who showers with his sister, who lie in bunks
and weep as orphans and convicts must,
they are silence in the back court, deadly
from the perimeter. They are sly jukes
and dishes, cuts and pivots. They are all
sweat, hustle, break, forgetting minutes, hours,
deaths they've inhaled, that well in their lungs
and lift now off bodies acrid and salt-laden,
lifting like the dust, red and hanging in the air,
until someone calls time and they're done,
and everything becomes what it was.

STACEY LYNN BROWN
Down South, all it takes / to be a church

Down South, all it takes
to be a church are some stencils
and a van. And my childhood
was full of them:

The Episcopal litanies of Sunday school
exercises in genuflection,
the low country Southern Baptist pit
of hellfire and damnation

hemming us inside the tent
while just outside,
flies hoverbuzzed above
plattered chicken, slaw, and beans.

Prophets profiteering in spoken
tongues as the Charismatic
wailed and thrashed and shook
their Babel babble down.

In dirt-floored shacks, fevered
believers danced themselves
into a frenzy, coiling snakes like copper
bracelets dangling from their wrists,

spit-cracked lips and boot heel clog,
the bass line itself almost enough
to give you back your faith.
Grape juice in Dixie

cups, cardboard host, backwashed
wine, this grit who'd been told
to be still and learn
was never any closer to God

than when I stood at the back of that
whitewashed clapboard A.M.E. I could only
ever visit: The preacher pacing the worn
strip of rug, pleading, *Help us, Lord,*

teach us how to love,
sending testified ripples that washed
over heads nodding bobs
on the waves of his words:

the choir rocking, feet stomping, peace
only to be found in the swing skirt of shimmy
and the big-bellied voices booming it holy
in the gospel of *move and you shall know* sway.

GABRIELLE CALVOCORESSI
A Love Supreme

You beautiful, broke-
back horse of my heart. Proud,
debonair, not quite there

in the head. You current
with no river in sight.
Current as confetti

after parades. You
small-town. Italian
ice shop next to brothels

beside the highway.
Sweet and sweaty. You high
as a kite coming

down. You suburban sprawled
on the bed. You dead? Not
nearly. Not yet.

Gabrielle Calvocoressi on discovering poetry
I had my first job at a little book store called Library Hours, and I essentially
asked if I could get paid in books. The first book I got was by Donald Hall,
Kicking the Leaves.

MONICA FERRELL
The Fire of Despair

To flux the snakebite I swallowed the whole
Vial of venom. Presently, vapored and fevered, I
Became the queen who lies on her lion-footed couch
Sweating into the light white sheet of day.

—Everyone is whispering behind a thin screen:
They speak of her *pulse*, her *signs of vitality*, her *blood
Pressure*, the awful bolus of its squeezing
Far too much red stuff into far too small a pump.

Now the fires are all gone out. For three days I have been ash;
On the fourth the slightest wind can blow me to pieces:
A scrap of a smile, shred of the has-been-girl clinging
Like remnants of a sail scattered on the blank sea.

MATTHEA HARVEY

The Future of Terror / 11

From the gable window, we shot
at what was left: gargoyles and garden gnomes.
I accidentally shot the generator
which would have been hard to gloss over
in a report except we weren't writing reports
anymore. We ate our gruel and watched
the hail crush the hay we'd hoped to harvest.
I found a handkerchief drying on a hook
and without a hint of irony, pocketed it.
Here was my hypothesis: we were inextricably
fucked. We'd killed all the inventors and all
the jesters just when we most needed humor
and invention. The lake breeze was lugubrious
at best, couldn't lift the leaves. As the day lengthened,
we knew we'd reached the lattermost moment.
The airlift wasn't on its way. Make-believe
was all I had left but I couldn't help but see
there was no "we"—you were a mannequin
and I'd been flying solo. I thought about
how birds can turn around mid-air, how
the nudibranch has no notion it might need
a shell. Swell. I ate the last napoleon—
it said *Onward!* on the packaging.
There was one shot left in my rifle.
I polish my plimsolls.
I wrapped myself in a quilt.
So this is how you live in the present.

RAVI SHANKAR
Spangling the Sea ⓒ

Ruffle and tuck, river fabric wags doggedly towards ocean,
Heaping surface on surface, its cadence a gown.

Perpetually beneath lurks stillness, a calm inseam sewn
By handless needles, distinct from yet part of the sequined

Design that glints iridescent now, then dark as pine.
Between silt and waver live many denizens of the deep:

Zigzagging shiners, freshwater drums, tessellated darters,
Grass carp, a kaleidoscopic plenitude that yaws and rolls

Among root wads and bubble curtains drawn on riparian
Terraces, hinged vertebrae whipping back and forth

In an elastic continuum displacing the fluid milieu,
Enabling them, polarized or not, to scull along in schools.

Nothing in outer space so bizarre as episodes underwater:
The gilled emerge from bouts of massive oviparity

Staged upon plankton columns where some fry turn larval
While the majority never leave the sure rot of egg sleep.

Whether due to snowmelt in mountainous headwater tracts
Or to rainfall from cumulonimbus fancy, for whatever reason

Water appears from serpentine soil and prairie-scrub mosaic,
A small muddy trickle that gains momentum as it swells

And deepens, sweeping along twigs, carcasses, bald tires,
To empty at length into estuaries engulfed by tides

Perpetually born of a body undressed in hastening garb,
Upholstering two-thirds more surface than any ground.

V. PENELOPE PELIZZON
Human Field

      Now it snows without sticking, the invisible
               air given a ghost's body by motes
fleet as the fireflies' sexual isotopes
          igniting the meadow with little half-lives,

      but colder. A starling flock, disrupted,
             ascends and circles twice in loose
precision, high enough to seem the very

          negative of snow: emphatic, demanding,
      warm-blooded, though their bones
             are hollow and their bivalve hearts
lighter than a sanded clam shell

          or the whitest pearl.
               Winter's revenant
   invites you into it, and there you lie
            while the bleached sheet, accumulating,
translates you to an angel in a solitary bed.

        Beat your wings to leave your signature,
    sole mark on the virgin manuscript.
           Or, still now, the figure weeping on a tomb.

What are you hiding from, in a body of snow?

      A touch and it melts on your finger.

    Because this is not your element, even if
            you learn to lie in it, unblinking, and watch it
falling from a bloodless sky,

      faster now, faster, till all the field is white.

MAJOR JACKSON
Leaving Saturn

Sun Ra & His Year 2000 Myth Science Arkestra
at Grendel's Lair Cabaret, 1986

Skyrocketed—
My eyes dilate old
Copper pennies.
Effortlessly, I play
*

Manifesto of the One
Stringed Harp. Only
This time I'm washed
Ashore, ship-wrecked
*

In Birmingham.
My black porcelain
Fingers, my sole
Possession. So I
*

Hammer out
Equations for
A New Thing.
Ogommetelli,
*

Ovid & Homer
Behind me, I toss
Apple peelings in
The air & half-hear
*

Brush strokes, the up
Kick of autumn
Leaves, the Arkestra
Laying down for
*

New dimensions.
I could be at Berkeley
Teaching a course—
Fixin's: How to Dress
*

Myth or *Generations:*
Spaceships in Harlem.
Instead, vibes from Chi-
Town, must be Fletcher's

    *

Big Band Music—oh,
My brother, the wind—
& know this life is
Only a circus. I'm

    *

Brushed aside: a naif,
A charlatan, too avant
Garde. Satellite music for
A futuristic tent, says

    *

One critic. Heartbreak
In outer space, says
Another,—lunar
Dust on the brain.

    *

I head to NewYork.
NewYork loves
A spectacle: wet pain
Of cement, sweet

    *

Scent of gulls swirling
Between skyscrapers
So tall, looks like war.
If what I'm told is true

    *

Mars is dying, it's after
The end of the world.
So, here I am,
In Philadelphia,

*

Death's headquarters,
Here to save the cosmos,
Here to dance in a bed
Of living gravestones.

UNDERSTANDING AL GREEN
Poems Written to Music

SEBASTIAN MATTHEWS
What Love Is

You could tell he was a Marsalis
brother, even sitting in the back:
he had that muddy river lilt

in his voice, the bristling intellect
and the irrepressible need to teach
the storied history of African-

American classical music. Jazz
was in his blood as legacy.
The *Funky Butt* was jammed, only this

back table free, whiskeys on the way.
A Basie number, Monk. The band
tight, Delfeayo's trombone aflame

from the opening chorus. I even
didn't mind that nearby tables
were more chatter than rapt attention,

or that our waitress took her time.
For Delfeayo was holding forth
on the subject of "cuttin'," that

fraternal pissing contest where raw-
boned skill and bravado run loose
to fight for the night's supremacy.

When the trumpet got introduced,
he looked over at Marsalis, a little
reticent to step into the ring.

Who could blame him? Delfeayo was all
over the bone: so low in the register
your feet could feel it; so high

he was bumping the night's rafters.
And not just range. He donned all the hats
of virtuosity in rapid succession

and swung like crazy, too. The trumpeter
was game, following behind
like a younger brother, tossing up

the bell of his horn, blatting out wild
roundhouse notes. But he was going
down. And when he managed a high

C, and held it, it came from his waist:
he'd been cut off at the legs. We
nearly jumped out of our seats, like

at some cellar cock fight.
At the break, heading for the john,
I spied a couple groping

in the dark hall; the woman pushing
the man up against a wall, kissing
him hard; his hand cupping her ass.

And when the waitress set down our drinks,
her breasts dropping like ripe peaches,
a cowgirl tattoo dancing on her arm,

I just about burst into happiness—
for being among friends,
for loving my wife, who

I knew was at home
in front of the fire, dog asleep
at her feet—and raised a silent

toast to the night unfolding:
to soulful music and to the grace-
ful glance of good luck's passing.

Later, when Delfeayo played
the loveliest solo on "You Don't Know
What Love Is" I ever heard

(heroin slow, each note laid out
like an early morning baker
sets out a rack of bread loaves)

the place got church quiet, drinks
clinking as we listened in
on a one-way lover's plea

into the grimy pay phone of the blues.
Before we left, the couple returned,
the guy's shirt back basted

with brick dust and sweat. I shook
Marsalis' hand on the way out
in that tentative way blacks and whites

do, half soul shake, half *how you do?*
and told him what I thought of his solo.
He gave me a look I couldn't read,

that I'd like to think registered surprise.
What do I know? Out on the street,
on the walk back to the hotel,

past a broken-bottled Congo Square,
the four of us picked our way
through the drunks—city still

bustling past midnight, sidewalks
slick from a streetsweep of rain—
jabbering about the prize fight

of a set, and I tried to
tell my friend something
of the feeling that had taken

hold of me, stumbling over
the words like a greenhorn
sitting in. He listened, rapt, happy,

filling in the last gap
of my music with a huge *whoop*
and then, steps later, *Wow!*

Wow! and we crossed over
onto Canal, heads bent in reverie
for all the night had offered up in its swell.

Sebastian Matthews on his composition process

I often compose poems while I'm taking a walk. Like a lot of writers, I use a
notebook, and if I'm out walking and get an idea, or a couple lines fall into
my head, I'll jot them down. Or, if I'm without paper and pen, I'll just keep
those lines, kind of worry them in my head a bit as I walk, see if I can expand
them into four or five lines. As soon as I can, I'll get to the computer, write
those lines down. And, usually, the poem falls into place as I write, and I'll
get as much done in that draft as possible, and then print it out, fold the
paper the long way, put it in my pocket and that night, my last walk of the
day, I'll read it out loud a few times, take some notes, and do that for a couple days until I've worked the thing to death. I'll put it away, and then see if
it comes back in a week or two, or the next month. And, if it does, and I'm
back in it, and the language is fresh, I'll put it in a pile of the other poems that
are working, that are on the stove, and see where it goes from there.

SEAN SINGER

Ellingtonia

for Edward Kennedy Ellington

1

...And the lamp caught fire
after he put a blue cashmere sweater over it.
Subtle as a Nance obbligato
on filmy violin—two brown curves *en passant*,
purflings ease sound out of the stank of violin parts:
      belly, waist, chin rest, rib, sound hole, pegbox, tailpiece,
rounded shoulder.
Ellington was an expert on them all.

2

_____

libretto

holy writ: Billy Strayhorn would wake up,
compose for four hrs. Would wake Duke

: *Blood Count* or *Ballad for Very Tired and Very Sad Lotus Eaters*
for example, & he'd bring his golden torso up,
& finish off the rest of the composition.

In the morning, after composing
      all night, Duke would open the closet

[Full of blue cashmere sweaters]
      & His Orchestra was playing the next morning:
Plucky, plugugly, pozzolana, porous, & perfect blues.

3

Daffdowndilly Ebullience   Daibutsu Ear   Damselfish Ectogenesis
Dardanelles Edge   Darksome Eiderdown   Demonax Ellipse
Desirous Empire   Doughbelly Eohippus   Dovetail Espalier

4

Salieri eavesdropped
Mozart playing a word-sex game;
just then the creamy, squeezing oboe
exalted-unbolted *Chimaphila umbelata* plumbed beautiful music
the color of blonde night: red plum jam
on pumpernickel: a Puerto Rican hermaphrodite
putting on pink lipgloss.

5

Wednesday night, Ellington, who
could forefeel the slightest discolored saxifrage
leaf easing between two rocks, heard
through a catnap & a halfdozen chewed
pencil tips, the babygreen, sweetpea Billy
exhale.

6

Blue, through blue dukedoms passed on to accept
That place which comes to each of us alone.

KYLE G. DARGAN

Piccolo BLACK ART

for the anxious among us

All our back-speak
tanned blue by a chiding
sun—nothing we did,
said, or asked of the day.
Within the [flesh] within those distant holds
—bodies almost living
lingua franca—all the smuggled tongue.
Within us, all the palaver stolen and run
against the grain of who we are
until sharp. Speech must prick
both ends—poison the kill
and inoculate the pred—to kill. *How*
you sound just brass and hymn?
How you sound just break
beat—no verse? Is there
one sound whole
enough to blanket-burn us
free, burn our *we* so dark
we cease to be it: no auntie,
no Rainy, no Robeson, no crunk,
no big band, no Amos, no acid,
no soul. How you sound: a moon phase
of how we sound: a permutation
of how [they] were collared
and syncopated, probed and muffled
like instruments. We play it—
Jim Crow's carcass
with holes to touch and blow,
torque the note. Must know
note whole before you can strike
and pin its wings down
in the grand book, give it name,
give it era to atrophy. How we
sound is a slow sunrise to the West.
It is not dawn yet, why worry
some shifting gleam cresting the avenue?

CAMILLE T. DUNGY

black spoon

Billie Holiday

baby you were meant to be home   you were
meant to be what I ain't never known   blue flame
done melted my song and you won't tell me
if you'll risk the curse between my thighs
won't give me more than the music of your fingers
strumming my slip's strap   your chest sings
to my heart's ear while your wicked wisdom works
its secret privilege   but you won't give me more
than your body tuned for walking out my door
hush now   I'm the one done let you in
here's what I've been cooking   what I scored
before you came   you brought me nothing
I ain't already known   I'm bright as a horn
listen   I'll blow you down

Camille T. Dungy on the form of "black spoon"
It's a sonnet from my collection of rogue sonnets, and they're very rogue-ish—none of them are actually rhymed, though I pay attention to syllabic counts in a majority of the poems. So, you might not necessarily look at "black spoon" and think that it's a sonnet, which is important to me, because they're poems about black people in America who make the best of what they have, and aren't necessarily what people think they are when you look at them on the surface, and they are full of pleasant surprises.

LATASHA N. NEVADA DIGGS
gamelan

talofa, wa´tsi hi`ya  `wa`ya

a`le   ya(na)se   kamama

e kala mai ia'u

        Laka, funky like a unicorn

could warn you
pero lingo gotta   switch

swiftly wa´tsi   hi`ya gv li

bubble your waters   tread your kingdom

tip-toe on your vertigo

                flip to stereo
            can you hear me yo?

u´di´tle´ga!   *u´di´tle´ga!*

lehelehe kino flow
lehelehe maka jingo
kino *u´di´tle´ga!* flow
lehelehe jingo

chico ma goon ngun ngun ngun yeah!
china ma orit chichi sai

tip-toe on your vertigo

                flip to stereo
            can you hear me yo?

pulelehua   wa´tsi   hi`ya   a tsv ya

a'le we´si   fire eaters

        rum-riddle   linguistic skittles
enchanted   shuffleboard
what you heard   extraordinary

running down to Singapore
Pele, whiti te rã!

gonna buy me a lavender labrador
Pele, `ga´ no´ lv´sga

        restore your confidence

        make it fresh

joy   pop diss beat

jawbreaker   broken e's   hawai'i

        goli:ga   Tsalagi

detsadoa thal'ami

u´di´tle´ga!   u´di´tle´ga!

chico ma goon ngun ngun ngun yeah!
china ma orit chichi sai

tip-toe on your vertigo

                flip to stereo
            can you hear me yo?

gadia   pulelehua

wa´tsi   hi`ya   a tsv ya

u ´di ´tle ´ga!   *u ´di ´tle ´ga!*

idadia   pulelehua

       wa ´tsi   hi`ya   wa `ya ah!

August 12, 2005
Harlem, hot as hell

LaTasha N. Nevada Diggs on macaronic verse:
"gamelan" is macaronic—written in two or more languages. With macaronic verses, I begin with a melody, some type of call and response that would be written entirely in gibberish, and then from the gibberish match the melody of the gibberish with actual words from various languages. From there, I began to create the other segments of "gamelan." The challenge for me was to create this piece that would be hip-hop in influence but also give light to languages that are rarely heard. Most of the poem is in Cherokee, and then other parts are Hawaiian, Samoan, some Maui.

PATRICK DONNELLY
Prayer at the Opera ⓒⒹ

I had already been weeping quietly
for half an hour at the Academy of Music
by the time Ulysses finally made it home
disguised as a beggar. He was begging
for his son to recognize him, to *know* him,
and the boy longed to, but a whole kingdom
hung on this, and he was afraid to love a fraud.

When the Croatian baritone
stretched out his hand to the boy,
quivering thin and lonely
on the other side of the stage,
and sung his name softly,
Telemaco, Telemaco, mio diletto,
it was as if the floor of the world
tilted the boy into his arms,

and because I thought I heard my father calling,
I thought all voices were my voice begging
You, who made it easy for me to weep:
lend the gift of tears
to a man my mother said cried two times,
when Kennedy was shot,
and at my birth.

CHRISTIAN BARTER
Poem ⓒ

With the hope yet of writing a poem this morning
I am sitting in the middle of the kitchen where
I can see from the window above the sink
the early winter light bringing the old oak
to magnificent relief and can hear
the radio's classical guitar asserting
itself and struggling to reach
doubt, and I am reading from *The Book
of Job:* "Is there not an appointed
time to man upon earth?" and watching
a spider descend by virtue of his own
guts across that oak shining
as from another earth and touch down
on the sink divider and make
for some attractive crevice. Just
being here . . . There is no such
thing, I think as I hear now Bernstein's
drifting violin above some kind of ground
that keeps giving way, a piece
inspired by Plato's *Agathon.* Beauty
is a call to labor. With the hope yet
of writing a poem smoothing
like a coin rubbed faceless, I
watch a single crow pumping
the blue he is the absence of,
working it hard until the black
of the last trees takes him.

Christian Barter on jealousy

Maybe it was Richard Hugo who said it: Only love of someone's work can conquer the jealousy we feel when we look at it. When I'm in the presence of a poem that's good, but that doesn't move me deeply, I'm more apt to feel jealousy. And when I'm in the presence of a poem that is in other ways superior to what I do but I'm truly moved by it, I become part owner of that poem and it doesn't bother me so much that I didn't write it.

ADRIAN MATEJKA

Understanding Al Green

When I was twelve, a wiser sixteen-
year-old told me: If you really want
to get that, homeboy, you best be bringing
Al Green's Greatest Hits. And if you ain't
in the mix by song five, either she's
dyking it or you need to re-evaluate your
sexual orientation. Know what I'm saying?

With those words, I was off—borrowed Al
Green in the clutch in search of that thing.
Socks pulled up to my neck. Jeri curl. Real
tight Hoyas jersey was nothing but regulation
and I knew I was smooth and I knew
I was going to be in the mix by song five.
The whole walk from the ball court,

the wise man's words echoed like somebody's
mama banging on the door: the panties
just be slippin' off when the women hear
Al's voice. Slippin'. Slippin' because Al
hits notes mellow, like the silk that silk
wears. His voice is all hardworking night time
things. Not fake breasts, but you

and your woman, squeezed onto the couch,
taking a nap while the aquarium stutters
beside you. Nodding off on drizzly days
when you should be at work. The first smoke
after a glass of fine wine you know
you can't afford. Nobody, not woman
or man, knows how to handle Al Green.

That Girl from Ipanema would have
dug Al. Her panties, flip-flopping right
there by the sea. That sexy passing
the Pharcyde by would have stopped to say

What up? if they were Al. But they weren't.
And neither were you, last night when
that woman at the club shut you down:

I got a man...blah, blah, blah. Hate to tell you,
player, but she's at Al's place right now asking
for an autograph and maybe a little sumpin-
sumpin. What is sumpin-sumpin? I don't know.
But Al knows. And I'm sure you've heard that old
jive about Al getting scalding grits thrown on him.
You have to recognize those lies because

he would have started singing and those grits
would have been in the mix, too. For real.
I never believed the pimp-to-preacher story
anyway. The point is, Al's voice is like g-strings
and afro wigs and trying to be quiet when
the parents are home. The point is Al Green
hums better than most people dream.

Adrian Matejka on the influence of rap in his poetry
What I tried to do was marry the things that I admire so much about successful rap music—like De La Soul, Tribe, Chuck D, Rakim—with the things
that are successful to me in poetry. That combination, if I could achieve it,
seemed like it could be a pretty interesting mix.

AMAUD JAMAUL JOHNSON
On This Side of Mercy

after Mississippi John Hurt

Some nights, I need to feel like the Sheriff's backstage
And a too-tough niggah, who I owe more money than what's
In my pocket, is standing out front, and I know my ass
Is too drunk or too slow to make the exit and keep my guitar.
When I close my eyes and palm the soundboard,
My fingers make a constellation, and my mind is all about
The last time with my woman; her nails strumming
My ribcage, how her name tastes, hovering in my mouth
Like a circle of smoke. Then the cry I let go, like a bird
Perched on my tongue. Then each chord, a new vein opening.
And then I don't give a damn about nothing, anymore.

Amaud Jamaul Johnson on how he came to poetry

It's hard to say when I became interested in poetry. In some ways I feel like
it was accidental. I remember being younger as a high school student being
very interested in politics and I had a speech class, debating, I was on the
debate team and I was really interested in speech and writing speeches.
Mostly because of the whole idea of logic, that you could put words together
in such a way to change or affect someone's thinking, to possibly inspire
them to action. I think if I trace poetry back to that early experience, or early
realization, about the power of language, I think I've tried to continue that,
and I've looked at poetry as a means of communication but also affecting
some kind of change in the world.

MATTHEW SHENODA

For Charles Mingus & That Ever-Living "Love Chant" ⓒⒹ

after Quincy Troupe

pluckin from real to surreal, and back again
your bass line shifts roots, gnarling trees into singing children
resurrecting tired bones into swinging feet
all the while ringing the song of your Afro-Asian roots
taking us all on the ride & fall of deep-space swinging
like the floating verve of "Bird" and those before you
you can wrap it all up in the dark wood of your hollow bass
make it sing like the quieting love of eagles mating in flight
break-down note for note you've paved the streets of reverberating
cadence, Mingus moving thru space with that four-string bass
creating the nimbus of atmospheric jazz & raining down smooth
      streaks of
love, chanting like two-toned whirls swirling through water like
      ripples
of come-back-home blues, gyrating instrumental geese flying
      toward
reformatory refuge of wailing bass lines & smooth-feathered solos
you've got love, Charlie, chanting with your outstretched arms,
      moving
strings like a slide-by grooving, tracing knee to inner knee your
      lover rests
at the echoing space of every last note, calling across for some
      thing more

Matthew Shenoda on the sounds of poetry

For me I always hear poetry first. It takes shape like an apparition of music
that then transforms itself into kinds of word-notes.

TYEHIMBA JESS

leadbelly vs. lomax ⑩
at the
modern language association conference, 1934

a costume.

dark overalls,

handkerchief,

and ugly-ass shitkickers,

clutched like gifts in his outstretched hands

chase the stink of mule dirt back

into my head. now he wants me

to wrap my music in a brown bag of coon

to give them *what folks 'spect to see,*

says i need the genuine look of farm boy

to sow blues' dirty fingers between their ears

i remember

fame's promises:

$100 suits is what made me believe.

an outfit.

new blue jeans,

clean head wrap,

some simple, old, sturdy shoes

are a proper field hand's uniform,

down-on-the-farm-familiar:

dressing down—it raises gods

dark enough to capture the authentic blues,

bringing southland to a crowd that

says they want to hear how it sounds for a black

to scrape heaven's dusty starlight out of hell.

to tally up

and close accounts—

$3 for the coveralls, and they were on sale.

$50 wing tips made me a convert. $1 for the work boots, sold at half-price,
$5 cigars helped seal the deal. and here, a handshake serves as contract.

like always, it's strange, but,
dog-tongued anger sometimes loathing
laps at my palms, bursts from his eyes,
shrinks my bowels pummeling me—
like a clenched fist striking 'cross my face

let's face it.

i'm parole on parade, i'm an ex-con's keeper,
wanted poster on a short leash, something I can't much forget
biding time beneath the law in this prison-choked country—
of a master i chose myself. i cannot absolve this man of
that faded rucksack of *yassuh* his greatest crime—the crime of race—
growing one load heavier binding us all to blood,
with each slow grin cutting through skin,
stitched across my lips burning through history

ANTHONY WALTON
Dissidence

in memoriam Thelonious Monk

You have to be able to hear past the pain, the obvious
minor-thirds and major-sevenths, the merely beautiful

ninths; you have to grow deaf to what you imagine
are the sounds of loneliness; you have to learn indifference

to static, and welcome noise like rain, acclimate
to another kind of silence; you have to be able to sleep

in the city, taxis and trucks careening through your dreams
and back again, hearing the whines and sirens and shrieks

as music; you must be a mathematician, a magician
of algebra, overtone and acoustics, mapping the splintered

intervals of time, tempo, harmony, stalking or sluicing blues
scales; you have to be unafraid of redundance, and aware

that dissonance-driven explorations of dissonance
may circle back to the crowded room of resolution;

you have to disagree with everything except the piano, black
and white keys marking the path you must climb step

by half-step with no compass but the blues, no company
but your distrust of the journey, of all that you hear, of arrival.

VII

CLEOPATRA'S BRA
Poems about the Body, the Bawdy, the Sensual, and the Sexy

DAN ALBERGOTTI
Bad Language

We fear to speak, and silence coats the night air.
So we are dumb, as quiet as the kitchen pans
hanging on their cabinet hooks. What words
do we even have? The root of *fuck* is as much
to strike as *to copulate.* And sometimes *ravish*
is *to rape.* But when you're ravishing, you're
beautiful. Strikingly beautiful. Other tongues
do not help. Try saying "kiss me" on the streets
of Paris. God does not help. The Bible is full
of prohibition. *Thou shalt not,* saith the lord.
No sounds like *know. To know* is *to understand.*
In the Bible *to know* is *to fuck.* What do you mean
when you say *no?* I think I know. I want to know.
Understand me. You're ravishing. I want to know
you. Strike me. Don't leave me alone with self-
knowledge and these rich, fruitless, unspoken words.

Dan Albergotti with advice to young writers
Read the literary journals. If you're sending your work out to be published,
read the work that's being published there. Why should the readers of those
journals, and people's whose work appears in those journals, care about
reading your work if you're not showing—to the Universe—a care of reading
theirs? So, for the good karma there of being in the conversation, be a lis-
tener, a reader.

ERIKA MEITNER
someone calls

men to her house
she straddles the roof
they alternate turns
coaxing her down
they wait in the street
which spins on its axis
the wind gets monotonous
with purring fumes
exhausted trails
of hooked alarms
bordello rungs extended

everything is red red red
and waiting

take this light (night-swim)
take this sound (wing-span)

traversing the acrobat sky
she is jet-propulsion
and shy with crowned stature
divines the *go* relay's
fast-bursting signs
a car starter coughing
the hymned power-lines
bellies of dogwood leaves
wielding their fur she is
armor-ready   hyper-aware
poised on the edge
like a zipper's pull

if the moon is a portal
a gate to the real
like panties like heaven
a palace of skin
her fall will unlock it
a finger running
her lover's spine

a key a bolt tearing
one gold tooth one
gold star at a time
from the sky's body
eternal partner in crime
the strings that hold her

all want no pain only
breathless brilliance bring

AIMEE NEZHUKUMATATHIL
Small Murders

When Cleopatra received Antony on her cedarwood ship,
she made sure he would smell her in advance across the sea:
perfumed sails, nets sagging with rosehips and crocus
draped over her bed, her feet and hands rubbed in almond oil,
cinnamon, and henna. I knew I had you when you told me

you could not live without my scent, bought pink bottles of it,
creamy lotions, a tiny vial of *parfume*—one drop lasted all day.
They say Napoleon told Josephine not to bathe for two weeks
so he could savor her raw scent, but hardly any mention is ever
made of their love of violets. Her signature fragrance: a special blend

of these crushed purple blooms for wrist, cleavage, earlobe.
Some expected to discover a valuable painting inside
the locket around Napoleon's neck when he died, but found
a powder of violet petals from his wife's grave instead. And just
yesterday, a new boy leaned in close to whisper that he loved

the smell of my perfume, the one you handpicked years ago.
I could tell he wanted to kiss me, his breath heavy and slow
against my neck. My face lit blue from the movie screen—
I said nothing, only sat up and stared straight ahead. But
by evening's end, I let him have it: twenty-seven kisses

on my neck, twenty-seven small murders of you. And the count
is correct, I know—each sweet press one less number to weigh
heavy in the next boy's cupped hands. Your mark on me washed
away with each kiss. The last one so cold, so filled with mist
and tiny daggers, I already smelled blood on my hands.

CHAD DAVIDSON
Cleopatra's Bra

It is one thing to uphold one's passions,
another to retain them. That thin seam
between impassioned and fashion: it could be

just another form of governing,
intimacy. Who knows if sequins spiraled
around each nipple, lapis clinging to straps.

Each mouthful of wine would raise her body heat
until a touch of gold slivered and rose
off her dark skin, caught somewhere

in a jewel of sweat. This is the Egypt
I imagine: pyramids, obelisks,
the Valley of Kings, and one torn bra.

Meanwhile, the Romans fashioned their parchment,
filled it with long strings of letters: *a*
for *ave*, *b* for *beato* (blessed), *c*,

of course, for *Caesar*, with no space between,
as to appear infinite. Augustus did try.
The old argument: *come home, she's bad news.*

But for Antony there would be no empire
cloven: a pregnant dream as he lay
again with her, clothes strewn on the ground

like artifacts of a forgotten city
under ash, and those two bodies caught
once more, together, for all of Rome to see.

Because it did end, Virgil says, in ruins
of a city, toppled towers, and one
fictitious Dido who let it all hang out

one Carthage summer so hot the oarsmen
gave up their fears, Acestes descended his throne
without bearskin, Aeneas loved and left,

Dido died. I like to imagine her scrawling
a message to the future regarding love—
flagrant love—and sacrificial fires

like those she clothed her city in one night:
Beware the Roman come to lie with you,
one hand heart-heavy and bound there

like the swearing-in of a city
official. Feeling her lover fiddle
with the clasp, Cleopatra must have thought,

*does everything come undone with this
one small breach of virtue?* One giant step
backward, she hears the inevitable

unleashing of the dogs, the centuries
head to toe in armor, and the lift,
they say, of a shallow wicker basket.

I like to imagine her calmly spreading
her robe, a leisurely cup of wine,
her fingers unclasping the bra from behind

as the asp negotiates the sea
of azure silk that separates them, empires
colliding, and the golden tint of scales.

MATTHEW DICKMAN
Love

We fall in love at weddings and auctions, over glasses
of wine in Italian restaurants
where plastic grapes hang on the lattice, our bodies throb
in the checkout line, bookstores, the bus stop,
and we can't keep our hands off each other
until we can—
so we turn to rubber masks and handcuffs, falling in love again.
We go to movies and sit in the air conditioned dark
with strangers who are in love
with heroes like Peter Parker
who loves a girl he can't have
because he loves saving the world in red and blue tights
more than he would love to have her ankles wrapped around
his waist or his tongue between her legs.
While we watch films
in which famous people play famous people
who experience pain,
the boy who sold us popcorn loves the girl
who sold us our tickets
and stares at the runs in her stockings every night,
even though she is in love
with the skinny kid who sells her cigarettes at the 7–11
and if the world had any compassion
it would let the two of them pass a Marlboro Light
back and forth
until their finger's eventually touched, their mouths sucking
and blowing. If the world knew how
the light bulb loved the socket
then we would all be better off. We could all dive head first
into the sticky parts. We could make sweat
a religion. We could light a candle
and praise the holiness of smelliness. Imagine standing
beneath the gothic archways of feet,
the gilded bowls of armpits. Who doesn't want to kneel down
and pray before the alter of the mouth?
For my part I am going to stop right here,
on this dark night,
on this country road,

where country songs come from, and kiss her, this woman,
below the trees,
which are below the stars,
which are below desire.
There's a music to it. I can hear it.
Johnny Cash, Biggie Smalls, Johann Sebastian Bach, I don't care
what they say. I loved you
the way my mouth loves teeth,
the way a boy I know would risk it all for a purple dinosaur,
who, truth be told, loved him.
There is no accounting for it.
In fact there are no accountants
balancing the books of love, measuring
the heart's distance and speed.
In the Midwest, for instance,
there are fields of corn madly in love with a scarecrow,
his potato-sack head
and straw body, standing among the dog-eared stalks,
his arms stretched out like a farm-Christ
full of love. Turning on the radio
I know how much AM loves FM. It's the same way
my mother loved Elvis
whose hips all young girls love, sitting around the television
in poodle skirts and bobby socks,
watching him move across the screen like something
even sex dreamed of having.
He loved me tender for so many years
that I was born after a long night of Black Russians and Canasta
while Jail House Rock rocked.
I love the way my screen door, if it isn't latched shut,
will fling itself open to the wind,
how the clouds above me look like animals covered in milk.
And I'm not the only one.
Stamps love envelopes. The licking proves it.
Just look at my dog
who obviously loves himself with an intensity
no human being could sustain, though you can't say we don't try.
The S&M goddess

who brings her husband to the mall,
dressed in a leather jumper, leading him through the food-court
by a leash. The baker who scores
his wife's name into the thin skin of the pumpernickel
before peeling it into the oven.
Once a baby lizard loved me so completely
he moved into my apartment and died of hunger.
I was living there with a girl who loved to say the word
shuttlecock. She would call
me at work and whisper shuttlecock
into my ear which loved it! The blastoff
of the first word sending the penis into space.
Not that I ever imagined
my cock being a spaceship,
though sometimes men are like astronauts, orbiting
the hot planets of women,
amazed that they have traveled so far, wanting
to land, wanting to document the first walk,
the first moan,
but never truly understanding what
has brought them there. Love in an elevator.
Love in the backseat of your parent's Chevette.
Love going to college, cutting her hair, reading Plath and sleeping
with other girls.
Sometimes love is lying across the bed
but it might not be yours.
And sometimes it travels into a hostile territory
where it's hardly recognizable
but there all the same.
I know a man who loves tanks so much
he wishes he had one
to pick up the groceries, drive
his wife to work, drop his daughter off
at school with her Little Mermaid
lunch box, a note
hidden inside, next to the apple, folded
with a love that can be translated into any language: I hope
you do not suffer.

KEVIN A. GONZÁLEZ
Cultural Slut

You narrow it down to three—
the first episode of South Park,
the first time you read Sharon Olds,
& the Field Day spent under the bleachers
with Victoria, your fingernails
becoming taxis of her scent, her pupils
disappearing like marbles into a grate.
At nine, you asked your father
about the rusted dispenser
screwed into the men's room at Duffy's
& Scotch sprayed through his nose.
You fingered the change slot
& fed it your pinball allowance
but nothing came out.
It was Sharon Olds who killed you
with *the father's cock & the mother's cunt,*
the cartoon probes & pelvis-spills
what shocked you, like Victoria's tang.
on your nails after tug of war,
the one you skipped, telling your teammates
your fingers were crossed *for them.*
These are the boulevards you cannot rip
from your eyes. There was the Lucky Seven
& Naranjito, La Chica Fuego,
a cigarette puckered between her labia,
loops of smoke twirling out
like an exorcism before a neon backdrop.
All this at fifteen, plaid skirts
cutting you off in school hallways.
Your father's invisible son, Pepito,
was a day older than you
& hit the buzzer shots you missed,
held his breath longer underwater.
Remember when you brought Victoria home
& your father said Pepito
had already fucked her? & your first time,
how she bled, & you thought
you'd murdered the prodigal son,

the condom drowned
in the eye of the toilet's undertow?
None of it matters. Not your father's
sagging gray lungs or the naive
objectification of your title.
You've narrowed it down to three—
& wouldn't we like to see Cartman
slugging it out with Sharon Olds,
& isn't Victoria a name you've made up
to protect the identity of C.,
& wasn't C. a slut
for skipping away with the Ethics teacher,
the cross on her necklace
swaying like a silver pendulum,
& didn't you buy her that cross
with your pinball allowance, which was
surely a bill cheaper than Pepito's?
When you first taught Creative Writing
& assigned a "How To" poem,
a girl with a tongue stud wrote
"How To Fuck an English Teacher
for a Good Grade," & her first line read,
"Write a 'How To Fuck an English Teacher
for a Good Grade' poem." Maybe
your mouth watered, & maybe
you read Sharon Olds to the class
& said, *if you can't write sex like this*
you can't write sex at all, & yes, you are
older now & going against that,
narrowing it down to three
though none of it matters. Not the cherry-
flavored-chapstick or C.'s number
in the phonebook, 787-4797.
Not your life, that instant between
the last seven & the first ring.
Not how you hang up & she punches *69
& you retreat from the accusing phone.

PATRICK ROSAL
Uncommon Denominators ⓒⒹ

I add up the times I've fantasized about
women I've seen but never spoken to
and divide that by the hours
I drive past cemeteries and add again
the weight of breath in your mouth
measured in the ancient Tagalog word for *yes*
—but the number always comes out the same

So I subtract the moon
and the smell of incense on Good Friday
trying to connect Planck's Constant
to the quantum moment between
a candlelit flick and the back of your neck
setting aside my 7 dreams of having sex once
with Tyra Banks who tells me *God*
You Filipino guys know
how to make love to a woman
and even if I tally the 10,069
channels launched by satellites
which have an asymptotic relationship
to the count of stones cast
from a sinner's fist raised
to the power of eight million punch-clock
stiffs heading home late
still the number comes out the same
and when a beggar pirouettes
along an expressway's center lane
swearing this won't be his last
cigarette (smoke rising from
the rust in his moustache) I suddenly know
the acceleration of a falling body
has little to do with slipping
a mother into the ground or
a whole greater than the sum of its parts

And if you ask what I'm doing
with 7 loaves and 4 fish multiplied
by the root of a dried tamarind tree

or the coefficient of friction
of a bullet on the brink of a rib
or the number of clips emptied
into an unarmed Guinean man
on a dark Bronx stoop I'll tell you
I'm looking for the exact
coordinates of falling in love plus or minus
the width of a single finger
lost along the axis of your lips

Patrick Rosal on the form of "Uncommon Denominators"

The formal strategy I used to compose "Uncommon Denominators" was just play, was the idea that I would take as much math language as I remembered, and would put it in a poem. The poem itself turned out to be a kind of love poem, and I just let the poem fly with this equation.

MARK CONWAY

Marginalia on Our Bodies

Not that evening, early, when
we begged for retro-rockets to slow
the turning of the moon
to mud, or the bitch
star to light the grounds
of new rendezvous, oh we liked it—
the selected pleasures
of that modernity.
I especially remember
secondary relics: the rasp
of your lips, saliva, the salt
flat of your belly.

Now we slip
toward vespers, singed
by a slight twist
of vodka, humming
in the clear velocity
that shoots us past
the nights when I was plausible,
and yours. Here we sit with snapshots,
nodding, pretending
to remember our regret.
                              Or, work
to work all over, in the following
light. We bank
on restoration by dinner,
an annulling thump of hunger...

and search again at midnight
on the cliffs
of your bare torso
for the scrawled marginalia left fading,
words we wrote, in tongues
and lip, into the vellum
of our younger skin. Beneath
your breast, I find crude
Sanskrit praising the gods we left

and the gods that left us,
singing.

    In the last night,
when workers come to gather us
as we were, they'll see
    the scars used to mark

where we'd been hurt
on skin brilliant
and eternal as tattoos.

KEETJE KUIPERS

The light behind her head, the bright honeycomb of the sky

At night his long body works above me,
late into the hours that make themselves
from dust, crafting the landscape out of midnight's cloth,
pulling Stockholm from behind the moon,
its blue skies rendered in Delft ink,
the cobblestone piers that part the water
at its glistening seams, and then the summer

evenings on the Hudson, a New York
he's making in my legs now, those runs past Ellis
Island, our lady of liberty swung out
beside Tribeca's ragged shoulder,
her fragile skyline shaped with dusk's gold filigree.
There are the deaths that terrify me still

because they have not happened yet. He'll wash
them from my eyes with Japan and all her
colored scarves wrapped around the limbs of trees
that forget themselves in blossoming.
Like the flowering corset that is the world
doing up her stays each morning, shaping
herself again to hold us all in semi-precious light.

STEVE SCAFIDI

Ode to the Perineum

Maybe the soul is only a small place on the body
        —Larry Levis

And maybe not. Maybe the invisible filament that flickers
        in the idea of the soul is the soul.
                Some hummingbird of the universal mind—
brightly colored, precise and infinitely quick.

And dull. It shouldn't be, in any case, as intimate
        as say, the perineum, that pleasurable
                one millionth acre
of nerves that lies between the asshole and the valleying

gradual beginning of our sex. No, the soul can't be that
        close by and so inappropriate
                that to speak of it now
is to cross over into the language of the body and of

the hidden crevasses of the body. Well, the hummingbird
        now floats over a rose although
                such a symbol for the soul
to be honest must include the microscopic blue turds

thudding lightly onto the grass wherever that hummingbird,
        for you, will pass. I prefer the taint,
                this prairie of pure desire
so secret even the body knows little of its power until quietly

reminded we buck like a horse on some Mississippi street.
        This deep true south of ourselves.
                Patch of the promised land.
Kingdom of the cartwheel and the lazy falling handstand

in swimming pools. I praise the carnival hairs sprouting
        there like trees Dr. Seuss drew
                in a forbidden mood
and I praise blue moons, kazoos and white hot rivers

with fiery canoes in that vision of scramble pleasure
       makes us live through and I praise
             this small place on the body
that might be the soul. Hinge from which our legs swing.

Tingling thing. Like the soft spot on a baby's head,
       this fragile holy span,
             must be praised now and then
with all the gentle force that words can stand.

TYEHIMBA JESS
mothafucka

missing consonants the raggedy way
a beggar or a bad-ass misses teeth,
it found the shape of our mouths,
snuck in like a second-story-man,
and laid claim to whatever adult or adulation lay inside.

sixth grade's paul daniels was one cray-zy muh-thuh-fuh-cka
for doin' push ups in the middle of detroit's meyers road
during after school traffic, daunting the cars
with a slow count to ten before he sauntered off the asphalt.
he was also the muddafucka you wanted on your side
if some shit was gonna jump off.

this in a town where even the mayor might call you
motherfucker, like he did the governor of michigan,
and then explain to the press
that look, it wasn't nothing personal,
ya'll asked me twenty times
if i thought the man was gonna
sign the budget, and i said
hell, ask the mothafucka yourself.
think *pronoun*, think colorful replacement for *him*.

and when motown's carl carlton said
she's a bad mamma-jamma
we knew the code he was speakin'
to us in the streets.
thanks for the alternative, carl:
one we can slip slide off the tongue in front of teacher,
one that even the sunday preacher might sneak into sermon,

but when it comes down to it, when the shit hits the fan
you gotta get all verb tense about it, and mutha*fuck* all the pretense
cause i'm about to act a muhfuckin' fool up in this joint.

i mean,
will the real mother fucker please stand up?
are you the devoted fucker of mother,
one who would stay to raise his kids
to be bigger, badder, better motherfuckers?
are you one who simply fucks our mothers?
one who fucks any mother in sight?
one who, by fucking, left bastards behind?
one who fucks his own mother—
one who could make themselves
their own bastard child?

and would you please tell us
why you always seem to boil down
to one simpler, smaller word;
another one we could fit in our mouths
but never figure all the way out—daddy.

JOHN POCH

The Tongue ⓒ

for Austin Hummell

The scriptures call it wicked, hypocrite,

the bridle turning the horse to war,

the rudder the ship to rocks,

cursing as it will before the wreck,

after the interception, during the bus ride home

where we tried the various fricatives

in the rebellion of our youth.

While one child's first word is *this,*

and another tries to capture

her mother's single words with her fist,

and yet another asks at bedtime,

Daddy, how much is night?

—my toddler daughter only sticks out

her tongue at the word *tongue,*

her small, moist strawberry of a tongue

she seems to eat when I reach for it

with forefinger and thumb.

She is an alien to me sometimes.

When she head-thuds the table edge,

her tongue becomes an alien in an alien

rearing its ugly tongue-of-a-head.

Paul Klee said he wanted all his life

to paint like a child. He did, eventually,

which is one reason we should have

Surrealist action figures. A man

across the hall has X-Files dolls
of Scully and Mulder on his desk.
I remember how, for seven years,
we begged the TV, *Please, Chris*
Carter, let them kiss, just once.
Our tongues wagged at the monstrous
interruptions: The Cigarette-Smoking Man,
The Well-Manicured Man, all conspiracies
against their love we knew was more
than friendship or fuzzy spaceship worship.
Their secret passion was sealed
like an X-file we knew existed,
forbidden, in a folder almost hidden
like a mouth and its tongue
that couldn't state the facts
but could taste the story.
Let me tell you a story:

In another life my daughter will speak
with her tongue, be a wife,
say *My name is Eavan, I do,*
I do not like them with a fox,
will kiss a boy on the mouth,
will fall, will fill a boy's eyes
with her eyes, her mother's French eyes,
sleepy, almost always moving toward this kiss.

In another life, judging by their names,

(listen to their names)
Fox Mulder and Dana Scully
could have been rodeo lovers—
one calf-roper, the other, barrel racer.
But here they were each week, one believer,
one doubter, both traveling toward the same
afflicted podunk town in some brown sedan.
So often, they looked at each other
as purely as the U.S. looks at Canada.
Then they looked away.

Out of the mouth proceed
both cursing and blessing,
both lie and utter truth,
and one late fall, in the thick of sweeps,
another episode at the edge
of the millennium, near the end
of seven seasons, we wanted nothing more
than the kiss between the two.
I wanted a French kiss.

CAMILLE-YVETTE WELSCH
Afternoons

Making love in the afternoon
stops the world. The clock
beside the bed reads a dazzle
of broken red lines, vying
for completion. The pillows
on the floor dare not settle,
their feathers suspend inside,
a bloat of anticipation. The phone
clenches the cradle, willing
itself not to ring, and the faucet
holds its single tear. Outside,
if a dog barks, the wind simply
swallows it until our bodies stop
and slide back to single selves.
Then, around us, the spinning
starts anew, as if the electricity,
suddenly restored, starts a record again,
the slurred sound of the world
gaining momentum until it sings and sings.

**Camille-Yvette Welsch on how she became interested in
writing poetry**
I became really interested when I was in college because it was really hard,
and it was never something that you're going to be good enough at.

ANNE MARIE MACARI
Little Church

On Good Friday you call from across country
to describe crosses pushed

in wheelbarrows, penitents with mouths full of rocks.

Don't pray for me, is all I can think, my old faith
crawling sideways over

the dry earth, changing shapes, refusing the vinegar,
the sad sponge. I'm trying not

to plan ahead for love's daily resurrections—love born, slain,

reborn in the rumpled bed. When are you coming home?
You can't know how a woman wants, can't know
how forgiving her breasts

feel when finally found under their wrappings

as if they'd been waiting to be touched but didn't know it,
or how the muscular hand

of the vagina keeps calling, *enter, enter,* no matter
how long it takes you

to hear, how it then
lets go, cupping

the spittle and milk. Some days my belief is
a pale thing, like when

the blue afterbirth of love hangs
so heavy, the mouth of love

limp and open with weariness. The flesh knows
this one thing, it practices

for its own demise as when

giving birth, in and out of pain, a voice said, *This
is what it's like to die.*

As for the scolding bells,

I try not to listen, I'd rather feel my breath
rising toward you, so distant

from me, seeking the stray hairs at the nape
of your neck.

What horror would it take for me to go back
to the old words, to kneel again—

instead I lean into my pillow, my legs
slightly open, waiting

for when we meet skin to skin, having
to decide who I am

now that my gods have fallen away. Sometimes
only touch can help me

when I'm released with a cry

and returned to my loneliness. See how
the bed is a little church where

we have given up and taken back, spoken
in tongues, worshipped

and worshipped, then lapsed each night,

into oblivion.

VIII

DEATH AND *TAXUS*
Poems Serious about Puns and Word Play

KAZIM ALI
Renunciation

The books were all torn apart, sliced along the spines
Light filled all the openings that she in her silence renounced

Still: her handwriting on the papers remembered us to her
The careful matching of the papers' edges was a road back

One night Muhummad was borne aloft by a winged horse
Taken from the Near Mosque to the Far Mosque

Each book likens itself to lichen,
stitching softly to tree trunks, to rocks

what was given into the Prophet's ears that night:
A changing of directions—now all the scattered tribes must pray:

Wonder well foundry, well sunborn, sundered and sound here
Well you be found here, foundered and found

Kazim Ali on his upbringing and becoming a poet
I grew up in an Indian Muslim family, so when we would go to the religious functions and listen to the Maulana speak, I would be listening to these services, and it was all in a language that I didn't understand, couldn't know. But, I had to be there, so I could hear the *sound* of it, and similarly, when we read the Koran, it was Arabic, and I didn't know Arabic. So there was a relationship for me between the sacred and unknowable that is really connected to language and poetry.

STUART GREENHOUSE
Cowrie Apostrophe

Let circumstance be breeze. At once:
shells rush, rub ocean, is it sure
or is it unsure? You are unsure
then sure. On shore, then are shore. Sink, shell,
not once as one but down to one ten thousand
thousand ones. Now you are thought
approaching thought. A thought that moves
like breeze, not surf—an end-slow
breeze near not. Once, inland,
where the breeze moves so, was ocean.
Once you think it through some
ten thousand thousand years, you'll understand
that, not vague or me. Will that be memory,
as-if-remembering a moist body-in-body accreting
ideas once home, once heaven settled
to routine, you, set longer
than that body's set of days, the shape which gave
you shape you gave shape to?
What are you now? What are you? At the edge
of permeant being, ages roll
your thought, you, down to its subsumed selves—
its heart is you, its trying
is what you think surety is: unsurely.

Stuart Greenhouse on the most pleasurable aspect of writing
The most pleasurable aspect is definitely when I write something good. By
good, I mean something that justifies the effort. And by the effort, I don't
even mean just the ten or twenty minutes of sitting down, or hours of revision, I mean the life lived up to it, which it is successfully the point of.

CAMILLE T. DUNGY

The Preachers Eat Out

Vernon Johns

There were maybe four of them, perhaps five.
They were headed, where? It does not matter,
only, they were not home yet, were not near
anyone who could have cared. So hungry,
they stopped there anyway. And when they heard,
We don't serve your kind, one among them laughed,
That's okay. We're not hungry for our kind.
We've come for food. And when the one waitress
who would serve them—she had children at home
and these were tips—finished breaking their plates
behind the building, he called her over
to the table. *Lady, my one regret*
is that we don't have appetite enough
to make you break every damned plate inside this room.

SARAH GAMBITO

Scene: a Loom ⓒ

If I emulate you, where would my rafters be?
She pulls out her voice scale by scale.
She thinks I do not hear her emotion.
This is a shock.

To make it more specific—*my people.*

Children are the imminent sojourn.
A maybe of love.
Brilliant persuasion from the stands.

I buy you a plate of expensive pears.
I cut the pear in ½.

January 8th   We eat a ½.
January 8th   Someone dear to me has died. Someone dear to
                  me has died.
January 28th   *Ito ay isang pagdasal para sa kapatid ko* meaning

He was unkind and she loved him.
He left her on the impended highway and she loved him.
He went away to the far country and she loved him.

I do not know the Lord.
But he spoke in a lovely way.
Created. Silvery citadel.

RAVI SHANKAR

Contraction

Honest self-scrutiny too easily mutinies,
       mutates into false memories
Which find language a receptive host,
Boosted by boastful embellishments.

Self-esteem is raised on wobbly beams,
       seeming seen as stuff enough
To fund the hedge of personality,
Though personally, I cannot forget

Whom I have met and somehow wronged,
       wrung for a jot of fugitive juice,
Trading some ruse for a blot or two,
Labored to braid from transparent diction

Fiction, quick fix, quixotic fixation.
       As the pulse of impulses
Drained through my veins, I tried to live
Twenty lives at once. Now one is plenty.

PATRICK ROSAL
The Basque Nose

I may as well be invisible
when Curtis says to Idoia his wife
That Basque nose
Let me touch that nose
and she lets him
and I'm surprised I don't
repeat him: *Let* me *touch that nose*
even though I've thought more often
of her chin—what I would abandon
to touch the line along
the muscle of her neck
to the small ridge below her ear—
a place which has no simple word
even in the half dozen languages
we choose not to speak in that room

Curtis—one of the most benign
men I know except for one
New Year's when he got drunk and vaulted
his six-foot-four Iowa-farmboy frame
over the dinner table to stomp
the gum out of some brute
pushing up on Idoia
But do you blame him?
The brute I mean
for blabbing anything
the liquor—he mistook
for muse—inspired him to say
just to hear Idoia speak—her vowels
thin cool and round as céntimos
dropped in a beggar's hand

I smoke on their front patio
Idoia stops in the kitchen
And I hold my cigarette
to the window between us—
how (for a moment) she purses
her mouth near the glass

a mock gesture too much
like a kiss for me to ignore

After dinner Curtis, Idoia and I drink
wine which gives me courage
to practice my Spanish I think about
the difference between saber and conocer
conjugating each verb beginning
in first person New Jersey familiar
So when Curtis gets drunk
and kisses his wife's shoulders
they both close their eyes and I'm still
muttering *I know...You know...He knows...*

APRIL OSSMANN
Infidelity (CD)

I never stopped to consider
its less illicit pleasures:

its syllables tumbling so readily
off the tongue, the tongue

slapping lightly, repeatedly,
the roof of the mouth, the mouth

left open, as if with expectation,
or in surprise, or song—this solo

which leaves you alone,
holding the final note.

April Ossmann on her compostional practices
I often write the last line of my poems first, and then figure out how to get
there, I think maybe because I have such a goal and future oriented personality. Also, knowing where I think I want to end up seems to free me to focus
on the journey.

ERIKA MEITNER
Quisiera Declarar ⓒ

The primary purpose
of this trip is the (check
the box) the yes business
of this peripatetic
pleasure trip is declared is
vanished is I almost
disappeared once to O-O-
Okalahoma with a
(check the box) a man I
fell in (____) with over
the business of close
proximity over the
roving (yes) phone.
Another time it was
a guy on a plane to
Bangkok. He got off in
New Delhi, got off in
Bombay, got off in
Alaska on the
refueling stopover,
left me with
fruits plants food insects
left me with
meats animals wildlife products
left me with
a hickey as big as
Chiang Mai, and a case of
continental drift. Shift
me one gear up (clutch) to
local, available,
single, potable. Drink
me down and don't worry—
I won't hang on like
typhoid or dysentery.
I own an imaginary
boyfriend extraordinaire:
tongue-marker, heart-breaker
and I am so faithful

and he's so invisible
I don't even have to
declare him not even
to customs officials
because I have read the
crucial information
on the reverse side of
this form and I have made
a truthful declaration.

In some countries
it is customary
to declare nothing—
the phrasebook said
to use the word
tengo, to use
the word *nada*.
The Spanish
I know is from
Sesame Street—
salida (exit).
Tonight I was
trolling the saw-
dust floor of the
worst bar in town
(proximity)
it was called The
Real Luck Cafe
or Earl's. It was
called The Double
Down. It was called
The Tip-A-Few.
Total value
of declared art-
icles: nil. But

I came home at
dawn and I would
like to declare
that I am not
a visitor I am
declaring that
I came home
a resident
the primary
purpose of this
I checked the box
(a citizen)
I swear I have
made a truthful
declaration—
(the primary
purpose of this
visit was) I
came home
to you.

Erika Meither on "Quisiera Declarar"

For "Quisiera Declarar," which means *custom declaration*, I decided that I
was going to try to write a poem that had only six or seven syllables per line
to try to get the lines to flow really quickly down the page. For some reason
all the radio stations where I was living in California turned over to Mariachi
music after midnight. And so I was writing to Mariachi music really late at
night, and I think some of the rhythm worked into the poem.

JEFFREY THOMSON
fabulous ones

This poem is brought to you by the letter C.

Cattle egret, Big Bird says, *cetacean*,
the word squeaking like wet whale skin.

Big Bird keeps it real—his thug-life strut.

Do you like giants?
Only the small ones, the boy says.

Chinese catfish, cassava, cassowary.

He's an intellectual, spends his days off
in coffeehouses, crossing and uncrossing
the long orange tubes of his legs, discussing

Chomsky, conditional freedom, and *Cervantes*

with anyone who will listen. He marches
against the war, a thousand people
at his back, chanting
Catastrophe, cruise missile, children.

Big Bird refuses to fly south for the winter,
puts on his scarf and heads out the door.

You can't fool me, the boy says.
I know Big Bird's not real.
It's just a suit with a little bird inside.

Jeffrey Thomson on "fabulous ones"
"fabulous ones" comes from a sort of political conversation I was having, in
my head at least, with Terrance Hayes. He has a Big Bird poem, and I
thought that was a great idea, and so I stole his idea, and I put it to use in
my own fashion.

DANA LEVIN

Quelquechose

You want to get in and then get out of the box.

form breakage form

—

I was in the fish shop, wondering why being experimental means
    not having a point—

        why experimentation in form is sufficient unto itself
                (is it)

But I needed a new way to say things:
        sad tired I with its dulled violations, lyric with loss in its
        faculty den—

Others were just throwing a veil over suffering:
        glittery interesting I-don't-exist—

All over town, I marched around,
        ranting my jeremiad.

Thinking, What good is form if it doesn't *say anything*—

And by 'say' I meant "wake somebody up."

Even here at the shores of Lake Champlain
        mothers were wrenching small arms out of sockets.

Not just the mothers. What were the fathers doing,
        wrenching small arms out of bedside caches—

How could I disappear into language when children were being called
        'fuckers'—
                by their mothers—

        who were being called 'cunts' by their boyfriends—

who were being called 'dickheads' behind their backs—

It wasn't that I was a liberal democrat, it was that
                bodies had been divested of their souls—

    like poems—

Trying to get in or out of the box.

And the scallops said, "Neulle idées que dans les choses."

And I said, "I'll have the Captain's Special with wedges instead of
    fries."

And everywhere in the fish shop the argument raged, it's baroque
    proportions,
            the conflict between harmony and invention.

But then a brilliance—

The movement of her gloved hands as she laid the haddock out
            one by one—

The sheered transparency of her latexed fingers,
            in and out of the lit display case as if they were yes, fish—

Laying haddock out in a plastic tub on a bed of ice,
            her lank brown hair pulled back from her face with a band—

Yes it was true she had to do this for the market
            but there was such beauty in it—

    she was the idea called Tenderness—

    she was a girl who stood under fluorescent lights making
            six bucks an hour—

and she looked up at me and held out a haddock with both
her hands,
saying it was the best of the morning's catch.

LAURA-GRAY STREET

Doorstep Ecologist

But it should have fur and sun.

Shaking the fern fronds, the small dog windeth.
She stands, forepaws perched on wickerback,

peering for squirrels. What do you do
with the no-longer-husband in the son?

With the you in the daughter?
I'd like something beautiful here,

something profound, not this untuned piano staining the wall.

Something exact, lineated,
scanning the low skies like aisles at the CVS,

as if birds were purchasable as envelopes.
There is bittersweet and aileanthus. There are herds of white-tailed
    deer.

No mammalian tragedy for black comedy to pick clean.

The ancient Egyptians thought all vultures were female, opening
their vaginas in flight to the inseminating wind.

Thus translated "breeze scavenger."

Root tangle and stem, and the buzzards mathematical,
sine and cosine, *pi* in the sky, the sky a drawer of wing-nuts.

Except that's what you hate about Nature:
all those numbers, bleary, smeared, our trading on them.

I admit the disingenuousness of snow, rocks, birds, clouds.
And creeks, all bodies of water. But if a sentence isn't a black snake,

why syntax and all its sinuous equations? Consider:

Sylvia was saving herself for marriage, but then there was *Art
in the Age Of Mechanical Reproduction.* So she lost it

in the back seat of the Eighties. He used a sandwich baggy
as a condom. Those were the days before Ziploc.

Forget rigor mortising, clutter of taxidermy.
Not eviscerated but visceral: roadkill.

Because it's a hell of thing to move a dead horse (the equipment
is hybrid trapeze, crane, tow truck—and very

expensive). Why not let it rot in the field?

Open season. Demolition.
Lo, the small dog curls into an ear.

Lumber and mortar and everything mortal.

Efflorescence with each bang of the dust mop.

SARAH GRIDLEY
Under the Veil of Wildness

1.

I call the main body, marker: a standing as if

in stead of. Or else a thing stooped down upon, and snapped. From
    branch I call

the main body, bramble: crescive glow from a crusted switchbox.
    On and off until a kind

of curfew comes. I call the main body, espoused. Line of symmetry
    inside, trench between

two lungs for the twoness of, the two-timedness of breathing. By
    oxygen-drawn sheerness

into red I call the branches to describe themselves . . .

2.

Looking quietly at a trumpet, its flared bell, its blackness
    encompassed by brass I said

     wait

at a black fruit in seas of prickers I said *wait*. A body is mainly its
    branches

     branca   claw paw hand   its tender

and untender branches.

3.

A wealthy sound in velvet niches, silver bedded with silver. Draw
    the curtains

for candescence, candlestubs in silver antlers. The sun coughs
    down

auroras, illumines branches of

extinction. Beneath the tree a childhood coffer, a peony and

an acorn smell.

CHAD DAVIDSON
Diva

The very veery this heart thumps for,
she seems a mere heartbeat away,
a buoy bobbing in a bay

on whose shores I sit tongue-tied
to the sound of a fishing boat
tonguing the soft-sand shore-lap.

It's March. And if I reel it in,
it is real. So to step in,
to swivel dingy oarlocks and plod

out nearer the buoy seems
the very act of throating a bird
as one might stroke a chicken neck

to pacify. Isadora
Duncan knows, or knew, all
too well this feather fingering

of Fate, both divas. Stay with me.
I am moving quite fast, sculling
by the buoy before I know it

is the very emblem of the veery
I would like each small chatty bird
in this narrative to be.

Stay with me, croons the buoy
Bette Midlerian as I scull by
thwartwise. Thickets rise

out of the shore muck starboard,
my skull now heavy with chirping.
Stay with me, and I'd like to

slip out and slide to the spout
end of that buoy throatwise
and risen to song. *This is weird,*

I tell myself, by which I mean
the Anglo-Saxon kind, which kills
the very veery my heart adores.

Heart, if you have the heart,
help me swing the dinghy round.
Or dive down, bottom-dweller, and throat

this minnowed moat crosswise.
Nevermind the albatross.
Divide the drink for the wan and dewless.

Chad Davidson on memorizing poems
I don't have all my poems memorized, but whenever I give a reading I try to
memorize the poems I read. And I do think it teaches you a lot about poems
and it's made me revise my poems in odd ways. And, I know Robert Lowell
said something like that, that he was giving so many readings and memorizing his poems and that when he finally came back to them in writing he
realized that he had been doing a lot of improvisational editing and he had
simplified things or cut out things that were hard to say, or Latin epigraphs
he had translated. So, it's a really interesting process to memorize one's
work and the work of others. It really enhances the poem on the page if
you've had it in your head long enough to understand it vocalized, rather
than just a textual phenomenon.

MARK CONWAY

The Past Described, As a Figure ⓒ

What were those days like? Remembering
is like remembering

white, or water. It's another resemblance,
the libraries packed

with broken metaphors, book after book filled
with "water is like . . . ,"

"white as . . ." When Alexandria caught fire,
the librarians burned like candles,

like suet. As for the manuscripts and their similes,
nothing was lost—it was like a fire.

GABRIEL WELSCH
Death and *Taxus*

Yews are old; in graveyards they tent
over the dead, their berries blood heavy
blackening stones.

In our suburbs they crouch as battlements
in front of ranches and bungalows
whispering "Eisenhower."

Their botanical call is the drum beat
of perpetuity: *Taxus baccata baccata*
Taxus repandens—

the beat for the oarsman to stroke over Styx,
the stone in the prow, his face like the pit
of yew berries.

Taxus, taxus, take from us our light,
the tilth of our soil, our fears,
our house fronts, our sorrow. Make it green.

Gabriel Welsch on his writing time
It's been about thirteen years that I've been getting up and writing from a half
hour and an hour every day before I go to work, before I'm polluted with the
language of administration, which I work in most of the time now. Increas-
ingly, though, I've been able to carve out time in the afternoons as well. The
morning times are very fresh, very new ideas, very unconscious in some
ways, observant, things that nag at me, I work out problems in a writing journal. And then the afternoons are more for revision, or continuous work on a
project whose parameters and identity have coalesced.

IX

IN THE ROMANTIC LONGHAND OF THE NIGHT
Formal and Informal Uses of Poetic Form

LUCY ANDERTON

Eve's Sestina for Adam

I wanted the blood from the lip you'd bite
open for me. I wanted the soft back
of your knee that glowed like an otter's eye,
the flag of hair you'd throw out through the wild
sky, singing praises to Him through the air.
Clearly put, I was not born to be one

more pretty poppy in that garden. One
more handful of fruit just for you to bite,
a patch of dirt where you could plant your heirs.
I was a song you had to put your back
into. The first born fairy. Artless, wild
and bare. And I wanted more than my eye

saw, more than the final glance of your eyes
after you pinned me. No—I wanted one
of your ribs. So I took it. Felt my wild
heart crack with arias as my nails bit
into your side, sliding my fingers back
out, waving that slim wet bone through the air—

spinning myself in sass and yards of air
kisses—turning my nose and loud-ass eyes
up to Him. And yes His fire split my back
as if He'd snatched from its cloudy bed one
virgin lightening bolt and threaded its bite
through my bold spine—as if I wasn't wild

enough. As if loving me was too wild,
too blasphemous an idea to air
in Eden. Who was I to need a bit
of love from the gold apple of His eye.
Adam, you helpless egg. I slipped you one
kiss and bled for us, but you were all back

and shoulders to me. Offering your tears back
to that giant nipple. Crying of wild
blood on your thighs. He only could hear one

side. So when that apple dropped through the air
I took it deep in my mouth and then I
saw that the bliss of absolution bites

straight through the heart of any one error.
So, yes, I backslapped Eden with my bloody wild.
But then—who gave you the Universe to bite?

DIANA MARIE DELGADO

In the Romantic Longhand of the Night ⓒⅅ

Let's kneel on gravel, take apart the lace
of fruit, and blade the wool of gracious lambs
who kiss hard and eat the changing face
of meadows. Late, the lark's a con of hands

that frowns aloud, spinning a tale free of green.
Let's break into picnics on the phone,
befriending boys who crack safes and win
ribbons for pigs that curry in the grain.

Let's soap each face that's locked in a bathroom
and slip in a letter written in the night's romantic
longhand. Let's fake it the right way, costumed
in the right light for the wrong person.

We say we aren't, but we're seeking the tricky
algorithm of travel, boys who wager swans first,
surviving on cobwebs and capture.

EUGENE OSTASHEVSKY
Alphabet for Tamar ⓒⒹ

A is for Axiom
that proved arbitrary.

B is for Binomial
whose terms never vary.

C is for Circumference
that goes around and around.

D is for Derivative
left to lie on the ground.

E is for *e*
(tautologically shown).

F is for Frustrum,
a beheaded cone.

G is for Games
in which all players lose.

H is for Horror
of the Hypotenuse.

I is for Identity,
when A=A.

What J is for,
I just cannot say.

K is another
katatonic letter.

L is the Lowest
common denominator.

M is for Moebius
whose head was all face.

N stands for Number
in the general case.

O is for "Oops,
I'm dividing by zero!"

P: Proposition
for which slapped was the hero.

Q is for Quotient:
"You guys smoked all the dope!"

R is Remainder
or so we hope.

S is for Sine curve
that reclines in the nude.

T is for Tangent,
absconding for good.

U is for Union
(what else could it be?).

V is for Venn diagram
which joins two, or three.

W is for Whole
that equals its part.

X is a variable
made up by Descartes.

Y is also a variable,
it transforms on the go.

Z is for Zero,
sometimes written as O.

HERMINE PINSON

Dolores' Blues ⓒ

my name is Dolores
sorrow is my middle name
my name is Dolores
sorrow is my middle name
if I hadn't been born
I wouldn't have nobody to blame

my name is Dolores
but my blues don't right no wrongs
my middle name is Dolores
my blues don't right no wrongs
took my eyes off the road
and a mockingbird stole my song

sing a song of sixpence
got my pockets full of rye
gonna stay right here in this spot
catch that black bird in a lie

my name is Dolores
sorrow is my middle name
sweet sun don't shine in my life
it rains and rains and rains

you got me where you want me
and that I can't deny
I'm running out of handkerchiefs
cuz all I do is cry
my name is Dolores
sorrow is my middle name
if I hadn't been born
I wouldn't have nobody to blame

my name is Dolores
I think I'll change my name
my name is Dolores
I'm gonna change my name
change my clothes and change my mind
and leave the way I came.

Hermine Pinson on "Dolores' Blues"

My middle name is Dolorez with a "z." It actually was Dolores until I changed it. I was working on this blues with friends who helped me to come up with some of these stanzas. It starts off so hopeless, that we decided we had to find a way to make it end well. With the woman feeling a sense of empowerment, with her leaving with her dignity, and that's how we came up with that last line of changing her name and leaving the way she came.

ADRIAN MATEJKA

Battle Rhyme for the Rhetorical Disenfranchisers

You're like the fat kid
offering up ho-hos,
one finger in the nose,

sweet treats exchanged
for friendship.
Or the little dog,

big dog ankle-yip aesthetic.
If you need ask who is who,
you validate pathetic.

Like a concierge
once he realizes he's just
a parking attendant.

A snappy tie doesn't
mean independent.
A snappy vest doesn't

mean success even if
your walk is what Dick Gregory
calls *swagger.*

Disrespect for your poetry
is a read-by:
line by line and posthumous

like appreciation for Kafka is.
Let me tell you how
your verse stands with me:

you, embargoer of poetic place,
you, fat cat at a soup line.
Since you take up page space

one undeserved iam at a time,
I've got no choice
but to backslap your verse

like Mister did Ceilie.
You better hope Shug
starts singing and distracts me.

Otherwise, everyone from here
to here will know
you're fraudulent.

They'll know you didn't go
platinum or win a Pulitzer.
You didn't reach Byzantium

or tap-dance to a Wurlitzer.
When real poets are writing,
you're in bed dreaming

Wilfred Owen's Anthem
but without the flowers in your mind.
Only the slow drawing of the blinds.

Adrien Matejka on "Battle Rhyme of the Rhetorical Disenfranchisers"

"Battle Rhyme" actually comes from Alexander Pope. He was an unbeliev-
ably scathing writer when it came to critics who were disrespecting his
verse; you know it didn't matter, he'd talk about their manhood, their family,
whatever it took to discredit them once they attacked his writing. And there's
something about that vitriolic instinct that I always admired. It's always been
a part of rap music—MCs beef with one another constantly—but there's
not really any similar call-and-response in contemporary poetry.

DOUGLAS WOODSUM
Melting

Being a glacier, I remember birth,
The waves of stars falling over the years,
White, six-pointed stars descending to form
My soul. On my birthday, it always snows.
Being the sea, you wait for everything
With motherly love. You eat continents
Of land, continents of ice. Your blue tongue
Catches snow. You taste like salt. You make sand.
I'm inland now, grinding the path that ends
At your door. I'll pause for weeks on the shore
Before I let go. You will let me in
Then begin to melt me down as I float.
Months later you'll ask me, "Do you love me?"
I'll answer you, "Does the sea love the sea?"

CHRISTIAN BARTER
Can You

Can you love the dawn and hate the day? I do.
"Addicted to the beginnings of relationships,"
as I've been told. And told. And told. The new
light looks as something else when it first hits,
something more like Catherine standing up
across a strangered room, that promising look
she had before the promises, still stuck
with sweetness to her face in my notebook
of pre-day ecstasies. I love the feel
of gray seeping into black—what it represents:
the casting-out that could occur—and the real,
truant world opening, before it grows dense
with light and the need for endings, setting free
that inkling some lasting love might come to me.

MATTHEA HARVEY
Ideas Go Only So Far

Last year I made up a baby. I made her in the shape of a hatbox or a
cake. I could have iced her & no one would have been the wiser. You
know how trained elephants will step onto a little round platform,
cramming all four fat feet together? That's her too, & the fez on the
elephant's head. Applause all around. There was no denying I had
made a good baby. I gave her a sweet face, a pair of pretty eyes, & a
secret trait at her christening. I set her on my desk, face up, and
waited. I watched her like a clock. I didn't coo at her though. She was-
n't that kind of baby.

She never got any bigger, but she did learn to roll. Her little flat face
went round and round. On her other side, her not-face rolled round
and round too. She followed me everywhere. When I swam, she
floated in the swimming pool, a platter for the sun. When I read, she
was my peacefully blinking footstool. She fit so perfectly into the
washing machine that perhaps I washed her more than necessary.
But it was wonderful to watch her eyes slitted against the suds, a
stray red sock swishing about her face like the tongue of some large
animal.

When you make up a good baby, other people will want one too.
Who's to say that I'm the only one who deserves a dear little machine-
washable ever-so-presentable baby. Not me. So I made a batch. But
they weren't exactly like her—they were smaller & without any
inborn dread. Sometimes I see one rolling past my window at sunset—quite unlike my baby, who like any good idea, eventually ended
up dead.

SABRINA ORAH MARK

Walter B.'s Extraordinary Cousin Arrives for a Visit ⓒ

When Walter B.'s extraordinary cousin arrived for a visit, Beatrice and Walter B. were in the bath reciting scenes from their favorite sentences. "What's that?" asked Beatrice, pointing at the thin white hands reaching in through the window. "Oh," said Walter B., "that's my extraordinary cousin." Beatrice and Walter B. continued to recite, but it wasn't the same. "Should we lend him a bicycle," whispered Beatrice. "Should I cook for him an egg?" "No," said Walter B., "we do not have time for his particulars." "Go away!" shouted Walter B. with a splash. "Go away!" Walter B.'s extraordinary cousin dropped his hands over the ledge like two dead flowers. "We haven't the time for your threats, or your untouchable thighs," shouted Walter B. "Can't you see we are trying to make a living here?" And with that Walter B.'s extraordinary cousin was gone. "Thank heavens that's over with," sighed Walter B., relaxing back into the warm water. "He has already cost me the earth." Six days went by undisturbed. But on the seventh day Walter B.'s extraordinary cousin returned. His thin white hands reached in again through the window. "What's that?" asked Beatrice. "Oh," said Walter B., "that's my extraordinary cousin." "I see," said Beatrice with the feeling that something like this had happened once before. "Go away!" shouted Walter B. "Go away!" shouted Beatrice "Go away!" shouted Walter B.'s extraordinary cousin. It was not yet time to drain the bathwater. It would be years before it would be time to drain the bathwater. And it would be longer still before it would be known far and wide that those hands were draped in accusations even Walter B. could not forgive.

Sabrina Orah Mark on prose poetry

There's this photograph of a Hans Belmer doll and she's open at the torso and where her navel should be is a wheel. Belmer's plan was to attach to the wheel a rotating disk lit by tiny colored bulbs operated by a button placed on the doll's left nipple that would contain six wedged-shaped scenes: a boat sinking into ice, sweet meats, a handkerchief dirty with saliva, and several pornographic shots. I often think of this disk fixed to where the doll's navel should be as the perfect image for the prose poem; there seems to exist a reason or a center on one hand and a spinning, decentered randomness on the other.

THORPE MOECKEL
Chattooga

You don't know how the aluminum pole will feel on a body that's been underwater for three days, and you don't quite trust that you can tell the difference between flesh and wood this evening as you poke and probe from a raft platform in a rapid paddlers call Jawbone. All you know is the color of the water matches its sound and there is a wolf spider on every rock you use for balance and there are men on the bank, kin to the boy, with pistols and machetes and they claim to have killed fourteen snakes. You don't know that in seven days the boy will surface in an eddy where a raft trip—yours—has pulled over to eat lunch. And you have no idea that your friend three years from now with a grappling hook and come-along will unwedge a college student from the slot below Left Crack, don't know he'll have to wait a week for the river to drop, that even then with the force of the water, the body will only come in pieces, and that when you ask him about it—it's amazing what we remember—he'll say the watch on the left wrist was still ticking. And of course you don't know that in five years, in the same year and month that a doctor will cut your firstborn from your wife's belly, a man will lose his daughter in Raven Chute, that after weeks she won't surface, and that he'll attempt to dynamite the river, try to break its jaw so he can recover her body, so he can bury her proper. This evening with the aluminum pole growing colder in your hands and the men on the bank starting fires, some coiling rope, you don't know what you know, what you're feeling, don't know that even if this man five years from now finds his daughter, some part of him will have to leave her there and walk into the water below Raven Chute just downstream where it's almost calm, walk in for as long as is needed—maybe a whole life—walk in every day, and bathe.

Thorpe Moeckel on how to approach poetry as a reader
The same way you would approach a new body of water you've just discovered. You don't dive right in, hopefully—if you do, hopefully you don't break your neck—you probably just look around for a while and savor the different things you see. You don't have to worry about what it means. Let it wash over you, let it cool you off, or heat you up, or whatever it does.

SHANE BOOK
Stark Room

In a stark room I knelt and reeling, felt the wooden floor.
Against losing I was leaning, praying you'd left behind
A long hair in the brine. Soft animal gloves protected my sores
From habitual picking and pulling. There's a stain on my mind.

Against losing I was leaning, praying you'd left behind
At least cigarette smoke. I waited in the dark, bent away like a lone
    nail
From habitual picking and pulling. There's a stain on my mind.
Your night laughter strung thick in the rafters like a contrail

Or at least cigarette smoke. I waited in the dark, bent away like a
    lone nail.
Pails of night walks, berries in bowls, the hidden door in your throat,
Your night laughter strung thick in the rafters like a contrail.
What if you'd ripped a breath hole in my long fleece coat?

Pails of night walks, berries in bowls, the hidden door in your throat,
I know I have dreamt none of it. The house has been empty a long
    time.
What if I'd ripped a breath hole in my long fleece coat,
If you'd secured a clipboard report of my truest, dearest rinds?

I know I have dreamt none of it. The house has been empty a long
    time.
Wandering the crown of any tree I was never more glad.
If you'd secured a clipboard report of my truest, dearest rinds
You may have noted my growing lump, my landing pad.

But wandering the crown of any tree I was never more glad,
A long hair in the brine. Soft animal gloves protected my sores.
You may have noted my growing lump. (Admit it, you're sad).
In a stark room I knelt and reeling, felt the wooden floor.

KATE NORTHROP

The Place Above the River

The house is empty and girls go in.
They drift through hours in the summer.
Across the river, music begins:

Love, it's summer. The closed homes open.
The docks are decked with lights. But further
the house is empty and girls go in

to light their lovely cigarettes; they listen
closely to the woods. Leaves? A slowing car?
Across the river, music begins

where wives are beautiful still, and thin
(in closets their dresses hang, sheer as scarves)
while the house is empty and the girls go in,

shimmering, to swallow vodka, or gin,
which burn, and to lean from where the windows were.
Across the river, music begins

and will part waves of air. *Now. Then.*
The season's criminal, strict and clear.
The house is empty. Girls go in.
Across the river, music begins.

Kate Northrop on "The Place Above the River"
I always remembered and thought about this abandoned cabin that we
used to use for parties in high school. I was writing down this description
of the cabin and, pretty quickly, this poem took shape. It became a villanelle, and I wrote the two lines that were going to become the two lines
that are repeated. It took a lot of revision of the poem but the shape of the
villanelle had really announced itself quickly. So in the sense that I didn't
sit down to write a villanelle, the subject sort of claimed its form and I
found that trustworthy.

RIGOBERTO GONZÁLEZ
Doppelgänger ⓒ⓪
for Omaira Sánchez

There once lived a girl who sang and danced even in times of sorrow.
She didn't answer to your name, but before her death she wore
    your face,

taupe bequeathed to her as well. Like you, she inherited her small
    place.
Such expediency of selection: the pasty stars collapsing to allow

the other constellations room to expire into brightness. But you
    needn't share
her fate. You can live an entire life without succumbing to a flood:

you can hum without gurgling beetle mud, you can sway without
    shivering
neck-deep in tin debris. But borrowed body, in time you must vacate,

let another take your space. Don't worry about whom or when
    since the girl
who comes after is already here, her breath the cold carnation of
    frost

on the window as you press your reflection to the glass. When you
    die
you'll kill the girls you used to be. As you live, you'll flaunt the
    genocide

like lavender, fierce blossoming of beauty and mortality. The next
    assassin?
She's the winter rehearsing its inhale-exhale through the invisible
    nose.

REBECCA BLACK
Cottonlandia

Little wheel
something gnarls in the blood
in our Arcadia of mayflies.

We make wine from muscadines,
little wheel turning inside my heart.
In January after the crop

floats to Apalachee
other cargo arrives—old men
boot-blacked before the auction block.

Shawl of cassimere, calamus-
root, one small revolver
on offer at Muse & Co.

Little wheel turning, gossypium
grows gossypium grows
along the roads.

Cotton alone does not spin
into cloth   the bridge itself
does not burn   little wheel

turning inside my heart
what's been must be storied
grist mill   cotton gin

what's invented   inventoried

BRIAN TURNER
Body Bags

A murder of crows looks on in silence
from the eucalyptus trees above
as we stand over the bodies—
who look as if they might roll over
to wake from a dream and question us
about the blood drying on their scalps,
the bullets lodged in the back of their skulls,
to ask where their wives and children are
this morning, and why this hovering
of flies, the taste of flatbread and chai
gone from their mouths, as they stretch
and rise, wondering who these strangers are
who would kick their hard feet, saying
Last call, motherfucker. Last call.

Brian Turner on being an "embedded poet"
Two soldiers walked up, maybe 19 years old, 20 years old, and one of them
kicked the feet of the dead man and said, "Last call, motherfucker. Last call."
And that really struck me. And that's how this poem began, as a witness to
what had happened. The idea of sort of being an embedded reporter is often
talked about, but I sort of felt like an embedded poet. And in many ways, as
writers, maybe we're all that embedded poet within our lives and in the lives
around us, and it's our job to not let those moments be lost.

X

SELF-PORTRAIT WITH SADNESS, WILD TURKEY, AND DENIS JOHNSON
Aubades, Elegies, Odes, and Other Traditional Modes

CHARLES FLOWERS
Aubade

I dial The Number, punch a code
    to enter the backroom,
where I create a profile,
    with a deeper voice & the curt
monosyllables of attraction:
    Cut, thick, top, hot, now.

Nothing seems more hopeless
    than phone sex on Sunday morning,
early, around 5 or 6 am, when the phone lines
    are crowded with club boys
tweaking home & middle-aged men
    waking stiff & hungry & alone.

Outside the empty streets shine still
    with lamplight & dew,
though in the city, it must be something
    else—gutter water
spreading its stain under the slow
    sizzle of random taxis.

As each man describes himself,
    this must be like the early,
golden days of radio,
    when voices were visceral,
each imagination shaping a different world,
    more real than its listener.

I come here to connect,

     if not in person,

then to needs that require anonymity.

     At twenty, I needed to know

I could be loved. At forty, I need

     to know I can be wanted.

I don't last long, shuffling the profiles

     like a deck of cards,

that spills, when gripped too tightly,

     to the floor, where a boy

crouches against a PHILCO, its voices

     beating against his heart.

Charles Flowers on "Aubade"

Aubade is formally, usually, a love song that takes place in the morning when the speaker does not want to depart from his lover. Clearly, in my "Aubade," there's a slightly different scenerio going on. It's not exactly a love poem, but it does still get to the heart, I think, of desire. It speaks to me about what poetry is supposed to do—there's an emotional connection but there's also, hopefully, a spark or some sort of moment where the reader is surprised. They think they know what they're going to be reading and then, suddenly, it changes. And that, for me, is a successful poem.

OLIVER DE LA PAZ

Aubade with a Book and the Rattle from a String of Pearls ⒸⒹ

The color of the moon bleached the tops of trees
and you left a book on the table, face down
with its spine reaching for air. I thought

the book might hate you for that. With my pre-dawn coffee
and mouth full of sleep syllables I whistled the title,
held the book in my arms like something would reach for it
and carry it to another galaxy.

I would go on preaching to windows
about how the screens needed replacing, or
how the dust motes settle the shelves. You were in agony

yet you would not speak about things such as age
and the body gestures that come to claim your mornings.
Neck-sure, arm-sure, I think about you and your book
coming to some agreement . . . some place of rest.

Though the mica glittered like stars . . . though you breathed
circles in the dark of your skin, you entered
a slow recessional. It was a kind of starvation,
knowing the dawn would come with its larks

and cars stuttering past your house. You in your bed
shut tight against the tide of sound refusing to believe
that the book held your world in such simple connotations.
A book is a book, you said.

I take that for granted sometimes. Perhaps
you were right to press its mouth to the table.
My imaginings sometimes take me
away from you. So morning breathes

in my ear like the mutterings of a book title
that I've forgotten . . . tip of the tongue.

Each room carried us from clock to clock. Each tick
an earful about ourselves. God knows,
the way night moves its shoes from side to side
or how day wrestles syllables from us in our sleep.

What am I trying to say? Dawn on the spine of the book
simply stood for you many years ago. I thought of the denim dress
you had saved for gardening. You had asked if I could

remove your necklace. I fumbled at the clasp
and touched one of the ridges of your spine
as the necklace broke and the days fell around us.

MATTHEW DICKMAN

Self-Portrait with Sadness, Wild Turkey, and Denis Johnson

The congregation is sad.

Their books of daily prayer look up into their sad faces from the
    long
thin fingers of sadness because a man they loved, a man who lived
two thousand years ago, died while his mother stood below him in
    a blue winter coat and trembled.

I wanted to be a priest when I was twelve.

St. Francis spoke to me on the playground the day Anton swung a
    bike chain, cutting Martin's lip in half.

He said—

This is the long and short road, the long arms of puberty,
and at the end of it
the wild fists of the Holy Ghost
holding you up by the short hairs.

I can't remember what I said.
I probably said pray for us
or get out of our way.

On the steps of his brother's house Carl and I read Denis Johnson
    and drank
Wild Turkey out of the same bottle so in a way our mouths
    touched, drew away,

and touched—

and he was tall
and he walked miles for a girl in reading glasses
and no one was ready for Summer to flip the short days into long
    days
like pancakes.

In this picture I am wearing a robe and lifting my hands up over
my tonsured head.

I am breaking the bread of the neighborhood
before Martin falls off his skateboard,
before Christ begs his father to stop,
before the congregation leaves the church full of—what did Denis
Johnson call it—

sadness.

DANA LEVIN
Ars Poetica ⓒⒹ

Six monarch butterfly cocoons
      clinging to the back of your throat—

    you could feel their gold wings trembling.

You were alarmed. You felt infested.
In the downstairs bathroom of the family home,
      gagging to spit them out—
             and a voice saying *Don't, don't*—

ILYA KAMINSKY

In Praise of Laughter

Where days bend and straighten
in a city that belongs to no nation
but all the nations of wind,

she spoke the speech of poplar trees—
her ears trembling as she spoke, my Aunt Rose
composed odes to barbershops, drugstores.

Her soul walking on two feet, the soul or no soul, a child's
    allowance,
she loved street musicians and knew
that my grandfather composed lectures on the supply

and demand of clouds in our country:
the State declared him an enemy of the people.
He ran after a train with tomatoes in his coat

and danced naked on the table in front of our house—
he was shot, and my grandmother raped
by the public prosecutor, who stuck his pen in her vagina,

the pen which signed people off for twenty years.
But in the secret history of anger—*one man's silence
lives in the bodies of others*—as we dance to keep from falling,

between the doctor and the prosecutor:
my family, the people of Odessa,
women with huge breasts, old men naive and childlike,

all our words, heaps of burning feathers
that rise and rise with each retelling.

JON PINEDA

My Sister, Who Died Young, Takes Up The Task

A basket of apples brown in our kitchen,
their warm scent is the scent of ripening,

and my sister, entering the room quietly,
takes a seat at the table, takes up the task

of peeling slowly away the blemished skins,
even half-rotten ones are salvaged carefully.

She makes sure to carve out the mealy flesh.
For this, I am grateful. I explain, *this elegy*

would love to save everything. She smiles at me,
and before long, the empty bowl she uses fills,

domed with thin slices she brushes into
the mouth of a steaming pot on the stove.

What can I do? I ask finally. *Nothing,*
she says, *let me finish this one thing alone.*

Jon Pineda on his favorite writing time
I like to wake in the morning and write before the day starts. It's quieter then, and for the most part, all of the chaos of a day hasn't really seeped into the writing yet.

RUTH ELLEN KOCHER

gigan: v.

i will not write you an elegy
big-mouthed woman whose breasts

hugged the microphone stand like some breadfruit dream
of nippled clouds, woman whose arms winged softly
into her armpits in a billowing flourish of skin's bounty,

thighs and ass enveloping the world
with their musked satin, whose teeth

tunneled through the closets of angels
revealing their gilded garments,

whose eyes blinked back the salty spray of sea.
i will not write you an elegy,

though your voice encompassed the world
in a raspy under-song's embrace, a diamond glare
of c-notes crowning you each time you walked on stage.

listen to the cardinal cutting a racket through my neighbor's pine.
hear his salutation, his winged confirmation of music un-stilled.

LESLIE MCGRATH

Corpus

If you can bear it so, be dead
among the dead. The dead are occupied.
                    —Rilke

After they washed my body
and threaded my arms through the sleeves
of a dress I'd bought in the thirties
in a Cuernavaca market, they looped a rosary
around my folded hands. A bloom
from the bougainvillea is tucked behind my ear.
I am dressed for church; I am beautiful
in death. Oh, the perfume of my hands
rises from me like prayer. I am gone, yet here
I lie waiting for the man
to come for me, to wrap and box me,
to burn what's left. Unusable,
this brittle spine, these still feet.
Unusable, these folded hands,
hands that tended, arranged,
wiped clean floors cleaner still,
hands that chose the melon,
sliced and served it, threw out the rind—
the unusable rind. These hands loved work,
what will there be for me now?
Life was work; death should be no different.

Leslie McGrath on "Corpus"

It was a poem that I had been trying to write for a year, and I had written many, many terrible versions of it. Then I first heard the poem "The Dog" by Gerald Stern. Stern writes in the voice of a dead dog in a ditch on the side of the road, and it is the most remarkable, moving poem I have ever heard. When I realized that as a poet I had permission to write in the form of anything, dead or alive, human or not human, that gave me the thought of actually writing "Corpus" from the point of view of a dead Mexican maid. And then I was able to finish writing that poem.

MATTHEW SHENODA

A Prayer for My People

That one day
we will wish
to be nothing more
than what we are.

That we will see
within ourselves
the liberation of nations, of concrete.

That we will understand
the inevitability
in the lines of our hands.

>   There is a war raging in our backyard
>   With it my sister's spirit burns

That the fire of my sister's spirit
will consume our enemies
& burn our streets clean.

>   There's a system of mangled necks
>   Whose heads speak with oracle tongues

That we should learn to walk
with wounded feet

That our eyes must be liberated
from their granite

That our hands re-root themselves
from the pools of acid rain

>   There's a river forming in the bureaucrat's head
>   Its water made from rusted milk

That we may understand this false constructed world
& know:

Holy things
Do not die!

Matthew Shenoda with advice for young writers
My advice to young poets, aside from all of the standards of reading and writing and honing your craft, is to live: To find the spirit within you, to find the fire, and understand why you do this. Don't isolate yourself from the rest of society like many artists tend to do but really engage in society. Understand the tempo and the rhythm of humanity and bring that to your work. Study your own history, understand knowledge of self and bring that to your work. Engage. Engage in the human experience on every level you can and bring that to your work.

SUZANNE WISE

Confession

I had my faults.
I had my so-called desires.
I remained open to temptation.
I argued with my colleagues.
I did not reach 100 percent
in my assignments. But I was no pry
pole, I was subsidiary. I was aspiring
to cog. I wanted to be a gullible
sheep or a rowdy-dowdy shepherdess
or a shamefaced sheepdog.
When I learned what I had to be,
I sat down on my luggage set
and wept. Then I unpacked. I decorated.
I raised the roof. I flew my kite.
I removed all the skulls and thieves.
I told my wise leaders where to sponge.
I was less than resistant. I was more than bold.
I was beyond naked. I was technicolor.
I was a brilliant butcher, an innovative
streetwalker, a saucy sales manager.
I knew a good stogy, a fine lace teddy.
I lived for love. I erred accordingly.
I assumed the world condoned my stunts.
It's clearer today. I was misunderstood;
I was in-the-know everyone else wanted
out of. Today there are no traces
of erasures, and no qualms, no real
wrongs. I made judgments for the best
and by the standards of the time.
Now that it's over I must beg
for attention. I have been robbed
of the limelight that comes with
responsibility. I can only imagine
how hard it must be for you
to believe me, I mean, to hold
blame. I mean, to be you.

RIGOBERTO GONZÁLEZ
Confession

Tell us again, father, about the priest who couldn't fit his fingers in
your mouth so you had to suck on the Eucharist as soon as it touched
your lower lip. His hand radiated warmth like a canine's breath and
suddenly the sound of a shirt coming off, and suddenly the door
bandaging light, the darkness flat across your body and nowhere the
merciful word for Christ. The nipples were aflame, but whose? Bleat
in the throat, Biblical goat that sniffs the sticky fluid of its spilled
death and what a betrayal it is to move through the world with a pair
of eyes only to have it end with the nose. Tell us, father, how it aches
to have a fat thumb brand its signature on the flesh—wound that
makes you tear into the pillows of adulthood. Spare us the nights of
grief, dear father, and warn us against the fierce desire of men before
we drop into that ecstasy again of having a bastard drill the twin
fires to our chests.

PAULA BOHINCE
Prayer ⓒ

Adore me, Lord,
beneath this raw milk sky, your vision
of silvery cream comprising daylight.

I've kept our appointment
in the barn, board after board of pine
hewn by us,

sit beside the pig we chose
for his mildness
who smiles, now, in his waste.

I abide by the chickadee
who stutters in, a little obsessed
with the mirrored chimes, her baffled image.

Our saddles, oiled on thick nails,
gleam from the walls like 3-D portraits.
Something must be wrong

or else you would answer—
my father in heaven who speaks to me
when no one else will speak to me.

Paula Bohince on the most pleasurable aspect of writing
Everything after the initial first draft feels pleasurable for me. I love taking a
very fragmented, sketchy, note-driven first draft, which is always written out
longhand on a yellow legal pad, and transferring it to the computer.

V. PENELOPE PELIZZON
Seven Penitential Psalms

1.

Pain's first casualty is proportion.

So my brother, juror in a child pornography trial,
Browses my shelves while the Easter lamb roasts

And, coming on Weston's nudes of his son
Paired with a text describing how Neil at eight

Is "moulded with reedlike flow of unbroken line"
—The exposures framed so the torso, Pentelic marble,

Ends with arm buds and the stem of the penis—
Slams the book and storms out

Shaken that I own such things.

2.

The damaged man licking sauce from his spoon—
Why do I feel stricken sitting in the same café,
Watching his unbridled relish in the mess?
He's showing me a secret I don't want to see.
The toughest shell conceals the tenderest meat.

My friend rejects aids to help him hear
Because they transmit chat he's never
Learned to filter out. How do we bear
Any sense without muting its tone?
The cuff of meat around the marrow bone.

3.

The clergy who rejected Caravaggio's "Death of the Virgin"
For showing the bare soles of Mary's feet
Could hardly conceive the Holy Mother
Straining like a ewe in labor with the Lamb of God.

Yet Luke writes that the inn was full and the birth outdoors.
A beast's entry. No bed for Heaven's Queen but a nest of straw;
The babe's head haloed but, if we take the incarnation at its word,
Breaching the labial tissue crowned in beads of blood.

The first mystery is spirit housed in meat. And the miracle—
That you love the brutal creature eating from your breast.

4.
"Nice day," she remarks of the glacier-sharp noon beyond the window,
"A nice day, under glass." Backhoeing a new well, her son's

Unearthed a Venetian Whiteheart, the beads-for-beaver currency
Once swapped here by the river, six glass nubs per finished pelt.

Resembling a drop of arterial blood, it's crossed three centuries
And countless palms to this snub of cotton in the vitrine by their TV.

He lets me hold it, and the red seed plunges me into a vitreous
Humor where we're all flecks floating in the eye of God.

Then drafts whistle through their window's glazing. Like glass,
My faith's both brittle and liquid, ever shattered or shifting shape.

5.
The devil, weeping for help, is plaintive.
He calls us by name and it's unclear what we should do.
I say "should," because if there really is a devil
Gulping in fevered sobs under the bed,
Mustn't there be a God who shut him in our house?

Are we to show pity for the pitiless,
Prove his nature to bite won't stifle our nature
To comfort his wounds? Or is giving the whimpering
Little fiend a blanket and cup of milk a sin?
Which hell do we want to burn in if we're wrong?

6.
There was a horse farm, long white paddocks, beside the railroad.
Can you see where this is going? Those horses were beautiful
    and—wet clover,
Loose fence posts—hard to keep safe. The day two mares and a
    gelding
Stopped an express (no humans hurt, train delayed while the track
    was cleared),
My brother slipped off to the scene. He craved blood, I think,
    because he'd
Reached the age that needs to feel beyond doubt that the world is
    real.

A boy, ten or twelve, on a bike; some horses; a train.
From the blue it comes back, and when I recall his crazy bravado,
    describing
What remained of the giants that once lipped apples from our
    palms, I'm surprised
At my rage: Who'd put horses there? Who a railroad? Who a boy?

7.
Such frenzy! All this fluster, no stillness at the root.
Always weeping, raging, driving backhoes, giving birth....

You love illuminated books because they're crammed, like your
Little verse, with busyness. You want the world's
Shards on velvet, so you've built a reliquary out of words.

Ach, peddler, you're no better than the friar
Hawking pig-knuckles as the bones of a saint.

You want a form that will hold the river's water
So it glitters, miraculous as tears?

First, smash the vial. First, swallow the shards.

SARAH LINDSAY
Lullaby After Midnight

The tallest elephant draws night down
in a swathe that unrolls and falls and folds
on her shoulders, doubles back, doubles again,
heaping its thicknesses into pure dark.

Safe in that velvet, elephants sleep on the ground
for an hour, and kudu on buckled knees.
Birds cover their heads; dusk-hunting snakes
compose themselves around full bellies.

Baobabs sigh and stretch their roots
a further inch into earth. Where people lie still,
dreams slip between the bars of their cages.
Even the animals back of the stars come out.

Now mist-drops touch and grow heavy enough for rain.
Now babies wake their mothers from inside:
Into a place so damp and dark and quiet,
they are willing to be born.

AN INDEX OF POETIC TRAITS

This index lists categories of poetic traits that contribute to the sonic quality and/or overall effect of the poems in this book. Each poem is listed in at least three categories. While this is by no means a definitive list, we hope it is a useful starting point for those interested in the mechanics of these poems.

Address

Poems in which the speaker or poem address a particular person, set of people, or quality. In particular cases also called apostrophe.

Allusion

Poems that make reference to a story, myth, artist, or artwork.

Anaphora/Epistrophe

Poems that employ anaphora, the technique of regularly repeating words or phrases at the beginning of a sentence or line, and epistrophe, the regular repetition of words or phrases at the end of lines or sentences.

Assonance

Poems that employ assonance, the repetition of non-rhyming vowel sounds in close enough proximity to create a recognizable echo or approximate rhyme.

Beat, Regular

Poems that make use of a regular rhythmic structure that is not metrical (e.g.: 4–6 stresses per line that are not arranged in metrical feet).

Consonance

Poems that employ consonance, the repetition of final consonant sounds in close enough proximity to create a recognizable echo or approximate rhyme.

Enjambment

The breaking of a syntactic unit across two lines of verse.

Form, Conventional
Poems written in or toward traditional forms such as the sonnet, villanelle, and sestina.

Language
Poems that self-consciously play with language at the literal and
figurative level.

Listing

Poems that make use of the quality of a list.

Meter, Regular

Poems with repeating metric structure (e.g., iambic or trochaic).

Punctuation, Little or No

Poems that lack or make little use of punctuation.

Question/Statement

Poems that pose questions and then answer them, or work in a mode of call-and-response or phrasing and rephrasing.

Repetition

Poems that repeat phrases, sentence structure, or ideas to create rhythm.

Rhyme, End

Poems that use similar sounds at the end of lines in particular patterns.

Rhyme, Internal

Poems that use similar-sounding words internally in the line.

Sentence Length, Long

Poems that use complicated and extended sentences to provide momentum.

Sibilance

Poems that employ sibilance, a particular form of consonance employing S or Sh sounds.

Tempo

Poems that vary the tempo of sentences, clauses, or phrases to metrical purposes.

A CROSS-REFERENCED INDEX OF POEMS BY TITLE

This index lists each poem in the book alphabetically with at least three relevant poetic strategies that lead to the success of the poem out loud and on the page.

à table: anaphora; enjambment; repetition; sibilance
After I Said It: beat (regular); punctuation (little or no); repetition
Afternoons: listing; phrase length (varied); rhyme (internal); sibilance
Alexander Leaves Babylon: allusion; assonance; enjambment
All Effect: punctuation (little or no); sentence length (long); sibilance
Alphabet for Tamar: form, conventional (abecedarian); meter; repetition; rhyme (end)
America, the Halleujah: allusion; beat (regular); enjambment; listing; repetition
Ars Poetica: assonance; consonance; forms, conventional (ars poetica); tempo
Atlas: beat (regular); forms, conventional (nonce); open vowels; sibilance
Aubade: forms, conventional (aubade); sentence length (varied); sibilance
Aubade with a Book and the Rattle from a String of Pearls: enjambment; form, conventional (aubade): open vowels; repetition
Bad Language: language; repetition; rhyme (internal)
Barrel is Surely Coming Down the Hill, The: enjambment; repetition; sentence length (varied)
Basque Nose, The: assonance; language; open vowels
Battle Rhyme for the Rhetorical Disenfranchisers: assonance; repetition; rhyme (internal)
Battlefield, The: open vowels; rhyme (internal); sibilance
black spoon: address; allusion; assonance; consonance; form, conventional (sonnet); punctuation (little or no); sibilance
Body Bags: form, conventional (sonnet); phrase length (varied); sibilance
Burlesque: anaphora; enjambment; language; sibilance
called: Eurydice: anaphora; enjambment; epistrophe; language; punctuation (little or no); repetition
Can You: enjambment; form, conventional (sonnet); meter; rhyme (end)
Chattooga: form, conventional (prose poem); listing; repetition; sentence length (long); tempo
Cheese Penguin: listing; repetition; rhyme (internal)
Cleopatra's Bra: allusion; enjambment; rhyme (internal); sibilance
Colony: allusion; assonance; consonance; rhyme (internal)
Confession (González): address: consonance; form, conventional (prose poem); sibilance; tempo

Confession (Wise): anaphora; beat (regular); listing; repetition; tempo
Contraction: assonance; consonance; language; rhyme (internal); sibilance
Coos Bay: consonance; listing; repetition; sentence length (long)
Corpus: consonance; repetition; rhyme (end)
Correspondence: address; assonance; open vowels; sibilance
Cottonlandia: listing; punctuation (little or no); repetition
Court of Forgetting, The: anaphora; beat (regular); listing; sentence length (long)
Cousin Drowses on the Flight to Kuwait: consonance; phrase length (varied); punctuation (little or no); tempo
Cowrie Apostrophe: language; question/statement; rhyme (internal)
Cultural Slut: address; language; tempo
Death and *Taxus:* allusion; enjambment; language
Dissidence: address; allusion; listing; phrase length (varied); repetition; sentence length (long)
Diva: assonance; consonance; language
Dolores' Blues: beat (regular); form, conventional (blues); repetition; rhyme (end)
Doorstep Ecologist: repetition; rhyme (internal); sibilance
Doppelgänger: allusion; enjambment; form, conventional (sonnet); open vowels; rhyme (internal)
Double Dutch: enjambment; rhyme (internal); sibilance
Down South, all it takes / to be a church: enjambment; listing; rhyme (internal)
Early Snow and Winter Comes into Kilter, An: address; allusion; assonance; open vowels; sentence length (varied)
Echocardiogram: form, conventional (sonnet); phrase length (varied); repetition; rhyme (internal); sibilance
Ellingtonia: allusion; assonance; beat (regular); consonance; repetition; rhyme (internal)
Eve's Sestina for Adam: address; form, conventional (sestina); repetition; tempo
fabulous ones: allusion; consonance; language
Film, The: address; assonance; repetition; rhyme (internal)
Fire of Despair, The: enjambment; language; rhyme (internal); sibilance
first sturdy bee begins, The: enjambment; listing; rhyme (internal)
For Charles Mingus & That Ever-Living "Love Chant": allusion; language; repetition; rhyme (internal); tempo
Future of Terror / 11, The: assonance; consonance; form, conventional (abecedarian) language; rhyme (internal)
gamelan: consonance; form, conventional (macaronic); language; rhyme (end); rhyme (internal)
gigan: v.: address; assonance; consonance; form, conventional (gigan/nonce); rhyme (internal); sentence length (long)
gigan: xi: assonance; consonance; form, conventional (gigan/nonce); open vowels; phrase length (varied); repetition; rhyme (internal)
Gone Before: address; listing; phrase length (varied)
Hello,: anaphora; epistrophe; repetition
Here, Bullet: anaphora; repetition; sibilance
How to Fall in Love with Your Father: enjambment; open vowels; repetition; sentence length (varied)
Human Field: assonance; enjambment; language; open vowels; sibilance
Hurt Locker, The: anaphora; question/statement; repetition

I am the Real Jesse James: consonance; form, conventional (prose poem); repetition

I'll Say It This Way: anaphora; beat (regular); phrase length (varied); repetition

Ideas Go Only So Far: form, conventional (prose poem); listing; tempo

Imaginary Numbers: anaphora; enjambment; listing; question/statement; sentence length (long)

In Praise of Laughter: assonance; rhyme (internal); sentence length (varied)

In the Romantic Longhand of the Night: assonance; consonance; form, conventional (sonnet); repetition

Infidelity: assonance; consonance; language; rhyme (internal); tempo

Invention: enjambment; open vowels; repetition; sibilance

Jorie Graham: assonance; open vowels; repetition; sibilance

Last Day with Mayflower: consonance; phrase length (varied); sentence length (long)

Late Autumn Wasp: phrase length (varied); sentence length (long); sibilance

Late Twentieth Century in the Form of Litany: allusion; anaphora; epistrophe; meter; repetition

leadbelly vs. lomax at the modern language association conference, 1934: beat (regular); enjambment; form, conventional (stichomythia); listing; rhyme (internal)

Leaving Saturn: allusion; enjambment; language; rhyme (internal); tempo

Letter to Cain: address; allusion; anaphora; form, conventional (prose poem)

light behind her head, the bright honeycomb of the sky, The: enjambment; open vowels; sentence length (long)

Lines Written Before the Day Shift: anaphora; open vowels; repetition

Little Church: address; enjambment; open vowels

Living On Nothing But Honey And Smoke: allusion; consonance; language

Love: enjambment; listing; repetition; sentence length (long)

Love Supreme, A: allusion; anaphora; assonance; consonance; language; repetition

Lullaby After Midnight: assonance; listing; repetition

Mangoes: beat (regular); enjambment; open vowels; repetition

Marginalia on Our Bodies: enjambment; rhyme (internal); sentence length (long)

Melting: address; form, conventional (sonnet); repetition; rhyme (internal)

mothafucka: language; listing; repetition

My Sister, Who Died Young, Takes Up the Task: form, conventional (sonnet); rhyme (internal); sibilance

Oakland Work Crew: listing; open vowels; sentence length (varied)

Ode to the Perineum: consonance; language; sentence length (long)

On This Side of Mercy: allusion; repetition; rhyme (internal); sentence length (varied)

One, The: enjambment; open vowels; sentence length (long)

Past Described, As a Figure, The: consonance; enjambment; language; open vowels

Phoenix, The: anaphora; consonance; repetition; sentence length (long)

Piccolo BLACK ART: assonance; language; listing; repetition

Place Above the River, The: form, conventional (villanelle); repetition; rhyme (end)

Poem: allusion; enjambment; sentence length (long)

Prayer: address; assonance; consonance

Prayer at the Opera: address; enjambment; sentence length (long)

Prayer for My People, A: anaphora; consonance; open vowels; repetition

Preachers Eat Out, The: consonance; form, conventional (sonnet); sentence length (varied)

Quelquechose: language; listing; sentence length (varied)

Questions for Godzilla: address; anaphora; listing; repetition; sentence length (long)

Quisiera Declarar: enjambment; language; tempo
Renunciation: assonance; language; repetition; sibilance
Scene: a Loom: language; open vowels; question/statement
Sea Watchers, Oil Paint on Canvas, 1952: assonance; enjambment; sentence length (long)
Second Ending of the Fairy-Tale: anaphora; assonance; repetition
Self-Portrait with Sadness, Wild Turkey, and Denis Johnson: allusion; enjambment; phrase length (varied)
Selling Out: consonance; question/statement; sentence length (varied)
Servitude: address; enjambment; open vowels
Seven Penitential Psalms: enjambment; form, conventional (psalm); language; rhyme (internal); sentence length (varied)
Small Murders: allusion; assonance; sentence length (long); sibilance
someone calls: beat (regular); sibilance; tempo
Song: address; assonance; consonance; language; question/ statement
Spangling the Sea: language; listing; open vowels; sibilance
Splinter Becoming a Burning Plank, A: consonance; phrase length (varied); rhyme (internal); sentence length (long)
Stark Room: form, conventional (pantoum); repetition; rhyme (end); rhyme (internal)
State of Virginia after Southampton: 1831, The: allusion; phrase length (varied); sibilance
Tar the Roof: beat (regular); rhyme (internal); sentence length (long)
Third Shift: beat (regular); enjambment; repetition
This Might Be Real: anaphora; listing; question/statement; repetition
To Certain Students: address; consonance; form, conventional (sonnet); meter; rhyme (internal)
to crave what the light does crave: anaphora; assonance; consonance; listing; punctuation (little or no)
To The Men Who Mow the County Graveyards: address; open vowels; sentence length (varied)
To Whoever Set My Truck on Fire: address; listing; sentence length (long); sibilance; tempo
Tongue, The: consonance; enjambment; language; repetition
Tonight I Doze: address; question/statement; repetition
Uncommon Denominators: listing; punctuation (little or no); repetition
Under the Veil of Wildness: enjambment; language; rhyme (internal)
Understanding Al Green: allusion; listing; tempo
Walter B.'s Extraordinary Cousin Arrives for a Visit: form, conventional (prose poem); question/statement; repetition
Way We Were, The: enjambment; listing; open vowels
We Lived Happily During the War: enjambment; open vowels; repetition
What Love Is: allusion; enjambment; open vowels; tempo
what the water gave me: anaphora; punctuation (little or no); repetition; rhyme (internal)
Who Says the Eye Loves Symmetry: enjambment; punctuation (little or no); repetition; rhyme (internal)
Why The Marriage Failed: anaphora; assonance; enjambment; repetition
Windmill Makes a Statement, A: address; assonance; rhyme (end)
Wolf: address; assonance; open vowels; sentence length (varied)

CONTRIBUTORS NOTES

Please visit www.fishousepoems.org for detailed biographies of the poets featured in this anthology.

LINDSAY AHL is the author of the novel *Desire* and editor of *Bliss* magazine.

DAN ALBERGOTTI is the author of *The Boatloads* (BOA Editions, 2008), selected by Edward Hirsch as the winner of the 2007 A. Poulin, Jr. Poetry Prize. He teaches creative writing and literature courses and edits the online journal Waccamaw at Coastal Carolina University in Conway, South Carolina.

KAZIM ALI is the author of two books of poetry, *The Far Mosque* and *The Fortieth Day*, and two novels, *Quinn's Passage* and *The Disappearance of Seth*, as well as the forthcoming *Bright Felon: Autobiography and Cities*. He is also a founding editor of Nightboat Books.

LUCY ANDERTON was the 2005–2006 writer-in-residence for the Virginia Center of the Arts in Auvillar, France, and she has represented Chicago at three National Poetry Slams.

CHRISTIAN BARTER's first collection, *The Singers I Prefer*, was a finalist for the 2006 Lenore Marshall Poetry Prize. He is a trail crew supervisor at Acadia National Park in Bar Harbor, Maine, and a 2008-2009 Hodder fellow at Princeton University.

CURTIS BAUER is the author of the poetry collection *Fence Line*, which won the 2003 John Ciardi Poetry Prize. He is founding member of the poetry collective 7 Carmine, and the publisher of Q Ave Press chapbooks.

SHERWIN BITSUI has been a Lannan Foundation Marfa Residency Fellow and a 2006 Whiting Award Winner. He is the author of the collection *Shapeshift*.

REBECCA BLACK is the author of *Cottonlandia*, winner of the 2004 Juniper Prize from the University of Massachusetts Press. A recent Stegner fellow at Stanford, she is Director of Creative Writing at Santa Clara University.

ADRIAN BLEVINS's *The Brass Girl Brouhaha* won the 2004 Kate Tufts Discovery Award. Blevins is also the recipient of a Rona Jaffe Writers' Foundation Award for poetry. Her second collection, *Live From the Homesick Jamboree*, is forthcoming from Wesleyan University Press.

PAULA BOHINCE's first collection is *Incident at the Edge of Bayonet Woods.*

ROGER BONAIR-AGARD is a Cave Canem fellow and co-founder of the louderARTS project, a two-time National Poetry Slam Champion, and author of the collection *Tarnish and Masquerade.*

SHANE BOOK's honors include a Wallace Stegner Fellowship at Stanford University, a New York Times Fellowship in Poetry, and a National Magazine Award. Founder and Executive Director of the International Writers' Workshop-Ghana, he is currently producing and directing the documentary film, *Laborland.*

GEOFFREY BROCK's first collection, *Weighing Light,* received the 2004 New Criterion Prize. He has received an NEA Fellowship for his poetry and a Guggenheim Fellowship for his translations.

STACEY LYNN BROWN's first collection, *Cradle Song,* was published by C&R Press in January 2009.

GABRIELLE CALVOCORESSI's first collection, *The Last Time I Saw Amelia Earhart,* was shortlisted for the Northern California Book Award and won the 2006 Connecticut Book Award in Poetry.

TINA CHANG is the author of the collection *Half-Lit Houses,* and co-editor of *Language for a New Century: Contemporary Poetry from the Middle East, Asia, and Beyond* (W.W. Norton, 2008).

SUZANNE CLEARY is the author of the collections *Trick Pear* and *Keeping Time.*

MARK CONWAY's book of poetry *Any Holy City* won the Gerald Cable Book Award in 2004. He is poetry editor of *Post Road* and director of the Literary Arts Institute of the College of Saint Benedict.

KYLE G. DARGAN is the author of *The Listening,* winner of the 2003 Cave Canem Poetry Prize, and *Bouquet of Hungers,* both from the University of Georgia Press.

CHAD DAVIDSON is the author of the collections *Consolation Miracle* and *The Last Predicta,* and the editor, with John Poch, of *Hockey Haiku: The Essential Collection.*

OLIVER DE LA PAZ is the author of two books of poetry, *Names Above Houses,* winner of the Crab Orchard Award Series, and *Furious Lullaby.*

ANTHONY DEATON, a Foreign Service Officer in the U.S. diplomatic corps, has won a "Discovery"/The Nation Award for poetry and The Campbell Corner Poetry Prize. He is the author of *Rhumb Lines,* a fine arts letterpress book.

DIANA MARIE DELGADO holds an MFA in Poetry from Columbia University. She is working on her first collection of poems.

MATTHEW DICKMAN is author of the chapbooks, *Amigos* (Q Ave Press, 2006) and *Something About a Black Scarf* (Azul Press, 2008). His first full-length collection, *All American Poem,* won the 2008 American Poetry Review/Honickman First Book Prize in Poetry.

LATASHA N. NEVADA DIGGS is a writer, vocalist and sound artist. She is the author of three chapbooks, *Ichi-Ban, Ni-Ban,* and *Manuel is destroying my bathroom,* and is the poetry curator for the online arts journal, www.exittheapple.com.

PATRICK DONNELLY is author of the collection *The Charge* and is an associate editor at Four Way Books.

GIBSON FAY-LEBLANC is the author of a limited edition chapbook, *Gaps in the Record*. He teaches at the University of Southern Maine and is Executive Director of The Telling Room, a non-profit writing program in Portland, Maine.

MONICA FERRELL, a former "Discovery"/The Nation winner and Wallace Stegner Fellow at Stanford University, won the 2007 Kathryn A. Morton Prize in Poetry for first poetry collection, *Beasts for the Chase*. She is also the author of a novel, *The Answer is Always Yes*.

CHARLES FLOWERS is founding editor of *BLOOM*, a journal for lesbian and gay writing and is Executive Director of the Lambda Literary Foundation.

SARAH GAMBITO is the author of the collections *Matadora* and *Delivered*, and is co-founder of Kundiman, a non-profit organization serving emerging Asian-American poets.

ROSS GAY's first book is *Against Which* (CavanKerry Press, 2006).

DOBBY GIBSON's first book, *Polar*, won the 2004 Beatrice Hawley Award from Alice James Books, and was a finalist for the 2006 Minnesota Book Award. His second book, *Skirmish*, was published by Graywolf Press in 2009.

KEVIN A. GONZÁLEZ is the author of the chapbook, *The Night Tito Trinidad KO'ed Ricardo Mayorga*. His first collection, *Cultural Studies*, is forthcoming from Carnegie Mellon University Press.

RIGOBERTO GONZÁLEZ is the author of seven books. His two poetry collections are the National Poetry Series selection, *So Often the Pitcher Goes to Water until It Breaks*, and *Other Fugitives and Other Strangers*, winner of The Poetry Center Book Award.

KEVIN GOODAN's first book, *In The Ghost-House Acquainted*, received the L.L. Winship/PEN New England Award for 2005, and his second collection, *Winter Tenor*, is forthcoming from Alice James Books.

STUART GREENHOUSE's chapbook, *What Remains*, was chosen for a National Chapbook Fellowship and was published by the Poetry Society of America in 2005.

SARAH GRIDLEY's first collection of poems, *Weather Eye Open*, was published by the University of California Press in 2005. They will publish her second collection, *Green Transistor*, in 2010.

PAUL GUEST, a 2007 Whiting Writers' Award winner, is the author of *The Resurrection of the Body and the Ruin of the World*, winner of the 2002 New Issues Poetry Prize; *Notes for My Body Double*, which won the 2006 Prairie Schooner Book Prize; and *My Index of Slightly Horrifying Knowledge*.

MATTHEA HARVEY is the author of *Pity the Bathtub Its Forced Embrace of the Human Form*, *Sad Little Breathing Machine*, and *Modern Life*.

JAMES HOCH received a 2007 Literature Fellowship from the National Endowment for the Arts. He is the author of the poetry collections, *A Parade of Hands*, winner of the Gerald Cable Book Award, and *Miscreants*.

MARIA HUMMEL is the author of the novel, *Wilderness Run*, and *City of the Moon*.

MAJOR JACKSON's collection of poetry, *Leaving Saturn*, a Cave Canem Poetry Prize selection, was shortlisted for the National Book Critics Circle Award. His second collection is *Hoops*.

TYEHIMBA JESS's first book of poetry, *leadbelly*, was a winner of the 2004 National Poetry Series. He is also the author of *African American Pride: Celebrating our Achievements, Contributions, and Legacy*.

AMAUD JAMAUL JOHNSON was a Wallace Stegner Fellow in Poetry at Stanford, and a Cave Canem Fellow. His collection, *Red Summer*, won the 2005 Dorset Prize from Tupelo Press.

ILYA KAMINSKY is the author of *Dancing In Odessa*, which won the Dorset Prize from Tupelo Press, the American Academy of Arts and Letters' Metcalf Award, the Ruth Lilly Fellowship from *Poetry* magazine, and was named Best Poetry Book of the Year 2005 by *ForeWord Magazine*.

GILLIAN KILEY lives in the Monohasset Mill artist community in Providence, Rhode Island. Her work appears in journals and in the anthology *A Best of Fence: The First Nine Years*.

RUTH ELLEN KOCHER is the author of *One Girl Babylon*; *When the Moon Knows You're Wandering*, winner of the Green Rose Prize in Poetry; and *Desdemona's Fire*.

KEETJE KUIPERS has received fellowships from Oregon Literary Arts and the Vermont Studio Center and was recipient of the 2007 Margery Davis Boyden Wilderness Writing Residency.

RODGER LEGRAND is author of the collections *Various Ways of Thinking about the Universe* and *Waking Up On a Sinking Boat*.

DANA LEVIN's first book, *In the Surgical Theatre*, was awarded the 1999 American Poetry Review/Honickman First Book Prize and went on to receive nearly every award available to first books and emerging poets. Levin has received fellowships and awards from the National Endowment for the Arts, PEN, the Witter Bynner Foundation and the Library of Congress, the Rona Jaffe Foundation, and the Whiting Foundation. A 2007 Guggenheim Fellow, her most recent book is *Wedding Day*.

SARAH LINDSAY is the author of two books in the Grove Press Poetry Series: *Primate Behavior*, a finalist for the National Book Award, and *Mount Clutter*. Her third collection is *Twigs and Knucklebones* from Copper Canyon Press.

REB LIVINGSTON is editor of *No Tell Motel*, co-editor of the *Bedside Guide to No Tell Motel* anthology series, and publisher of No Tell Books. She is author of *Your Ten Favorite Words* and *Pterodactyls Soar Again*, and co-author, with Ravi Shankar, of *Wanton Textiles*.

ANNE MARIE MACARI is the author of the collections *Ivory Cradle*, which won the 2000 American Poetry Review/Honickman First Book Prize; *Gloryland* (Alice James Books, 2005), and *She Heads Into the Wilderness* (Autumn House Press, 2008).

SARAH MANGUSO is the author of the memoir *The Two Kinds of Decay*, the story collection *Hard to Admit* and *Harder to Escape*, and the poetry collections *Siste Viator* and *The Captain Lands in Paradise*.

SABRINA ORAH MARK is the author of *The Babies*, a collection of prose poems.

CATE MARVIN's first book of poems, *World's Tallest Disaster*, was awarded the 2000 Kathryn A. Morton Prize. Her second collection is *Fragment of the Head of a Queen*. She is co-editor of the anthology *Legitimate Dangers: American Poets of the New Century*, and is a 2007 Whiting Writers' Award winner.

ADRIAN MATEJKA's first collection of poems, *The Devil's Garden*, was published by Alice James Books. His second collection, *Mixology*, was a winner of the 2008 National Poetry Series and will be published by Penguin Books in 2009.

CHARLOTTE MATTHEWS is the author of the poetry collections *Green Stars* and *Still Enough to Be Dreaming*, and received the 2007 Fellowship of Southern Poets Best New Poet Award.

SEBASTIAN MATTHEWS edits the journal *Rivendell*; is author of the memoir, *In My Father's Footsteps*; and co-editor, with Stanley Plumly, of *Search Party: Collected Poems of William Matthews*. He is author of the chapbook *Coming to Flood*, and the full-length poetry collection *We Generous*.

LESLIE MCGRATH won the 2004 Nimrod/Hardman Pablo Neruda Prize for Poetry and was a Pushcart Prize nominee. Her chapbook, *Toward Anguish*, won the 2007 Philbrick Poetry Award.

MICHAEL MCGRIFF won the 2005 Ruth Lilly Fellowship from *Poetry* magazine. He is author of the chapbook *Choke*, and the collection *Dismantling the Hills*, which won the 2007 Agnes Lynch Starrett Poetry Prize from the University of Pittsburgh Press.

ERIKA MEITNER's first book, *Inventory at the All-Night Drugstore*, won the 2002 Anhinga Prize for Poetry.

SARAH MESSER is author of the memoir *Red House: Being a Mostly Accurate Account of New England's Oldest Continuously Lived-In House* and the poetry collection *Bandit Letters*.

THORPE MOECKEL's two full-length poetry collections are *Odd Botany*, which won the Gerald Cable Book Award in 2002, and *Making a Map of the River*.

AIMEE NEZHUKUMATATHIL is the author of *At the Drive-In Volcano* (Tupelo Press, 2007), winner of the Balcones Prize, and *Miracle Fruit* (Tupelo Press, 2003), winner of the ForeWord Magazine Poetry Book of the Year and the Global Filipino Literary Award. She is associate professor of English at SUNY-Fredonia where she was awarded a Chancellor's Medal of Excellence.

KATE NORTHROP's first collection, *Back Through Interruption*, won the Wick Poetry Award. Her second collection, *Things Are Disappearing Here*, was a *New York Times Book Review* Editor's Choice and a finalist for the James Laughlin award.

APRIL OSSMANN is the author of *Anxious Music* and winner of the 2000 Prairie Schooner Reader's Choice Award.

EUGENE OSTASHEVSKY's books of poetry include *Iterature*; *Infinite Recursor Or The Bride of DJ Spinoza*; and *Enter Morris Imposternak, Pursued by Ironies*. He is editor of *OBERIU: An Anthology of Russian Absurdism*.

GREGORY PARDLO is author of a volume of translations from the Danish poet Niels Lyngsoe, *Pencil of Rays and Spiked Mace*. His first book of poems, *Totem*, won the 2007 American Poetry Review/Honickman First Book Prize in Poetry.

V. PENELOPE PELIZZON's first poetry collection, *Nostos*, won the Hollis Summers Prize and the Poetry Society of America's 2001 Norma Farber First Book Award. Other honors include a "Discovery"/The Nation Award, The Kenneth Rexroth Translation Award, the Campbell Corner Poetry Prize, and a Lannan Writing Residency Fellowship in Poetry.

JON PINEDA is the author of the poetry collections *Birthmark*, winner of the Crab Orchard Award Series in Poetry Open Competition, and *The Translator's Diary*, winner of the 2007 Green Rose Prize. His memoir, *Sleep in Me*, is forthcoming in 2010 from the University of Nebraska Press.

HERMINE PINSON, a native of Beaumont, Texas, is the author of three collections of poetry, *Ashe; Mama Yetta and Other Poems;* and *Dolores is Blue/Dolorez is Blues*.

JOHN POCH'S first collection of poetry is *Poems*. His second, *Two Men Fighting with a Knife*, was the 2008 Donald Justice Poetry Prize winner. He is the editor, with Chad Davidson, of *Hockey Haiku: The Essential Collection* and is editor of *32 Poems Magazine*.

DAVID RODERICK's first book, *Blue Colonial*, won the 2006 The American Poetry Review/Honickman First Book Prize in Poetry.

PATRICK ROSAL is the author of *Uprock Headspin Scramble and Dive*, finalist for the Asian-American Writers' Workshop Literary Awards and winner of the AAWW Member's Choice Award. His second collection is *My American Kundiman*.

STEVE SCAFIDI is author of *Sparks from a Nine-Pound Hammer*, winner of the Larry Levis Reading Prize, and *For Love of Common Words*.

RAVI SHANKAR is poet-in-residence at Central Connecticut State University and editor of the online journal *Drunken Boat*. His first book of poems is *Instrumentality*, finalist for the 2005 Connecticut Book Awards, and he is the co-editor of *Language for a New Century: Contemporary Poetry from the Middle East, Asia, and Beyond* (W.W. Norton, 2008).

MATTHEW SHENODA's debut collection, *Somewhere Else*, was winner of a 2006 American Book Award. His latest collection, *Seasons of Lotus, Seasons of Bone*, will be published in 2009 by BOA Editions.

EVIE SHOCKLEY is the author of a chapbook, *The Gorgon Goddess*, and the collection *a half-red sea* (Carolina Wren Press).

SEAN SINGER's first book, *Discography*, won the 2001 Yale Series of Younger Poets Prize, and the Norma Farber First Book Award from the Poetry Society of America.

TRACY K. SMITH is the author of *The Body's Question*, winner of the 2002 Cave Canem Poetry Prize, and *Duende*, which won the 2006 James Laughlin Award of the Academy of American Poets. She is a recipient of a 2004 Rona Jaffe Writers Award, and a 2005 Whiting Writers' Award.

LAURA-GRAY STREET has received fellowships and awards from the Virginia Commission for the Arts, the Southern Women Writers Conference, and the Virginia Center for the Creative arts.

BRIAN TURNER's debut collection, *Here, Bullet*, won the 2005 Beatrice Hawley Award from Alice James Books, among other prizes, including the 2007 Poets' Prize. Turner was the recipient of a 2006 Lannan Literary Fellowship and a 2007 National Endowment for the Arts Literature Fellowship in Poetry.

ANTHONY WALTON is the author of a chapbook of poems, *Cricket Weather*, and with Michael Harper edited *Every Shut Eye Ain't Asleep: An Anthology of Poetry by African Americans Since 1945*, and *The Vintage Book of African American Poetry*. He is also the author of the memoir *Mississippi: An American Journey*, and with Kareem Abdul Jabar, *Brothers in Arms: The Epic Story of the 761st Tank Battalion, WWII's Forgotten Heroes*.

CAMILLE-YVETTE WELSCH is a senior lecturer in English at the Pennsylvania State University and the co-director of the Red Weather Reading Series and Penn State's Summer Creative Writing Conference for High School Students.

GABRIEL WELSCH's first collection of poems is *Dirt and All Its Dense Labor*. He is assistant vice president of marketing at Juniata College.

ELIOT KHALIL WILSON's first collection of poems, *The Saint of Letting Small Fish Go*, won the 2003 Cleveland State Poetry Prize.

SUZANNE WISE is the author of the poetry collection *The Kingdom of the Subjunctive*.

DOUGLAS WOODSUM teaches high school English in rural Maine.

ACKNOWLEDGMENTS

For their assistance and support, we would like to thank Willis Barnstone, Alison Bennie, Ray Black, Robert Cording, Robert Denton, Jennifer Eriksen, Elise Gaisson, Rigoberto González, Lola Haskins, Ted Helberg, Ilya Kaminski, James Kelley, Casey Latter, Alesia and Fay O'Donnell, Tim and Cheryl O'Donnell, April Ossmann, Ira Sadoff, Stephanie Smith, Gerald Stern, Cindy Stocks, and Emily Warn.

Thanks, too, to our colleagues and students at Bowdoin College, San Francisco State University, and the University of Maine Farmington.

Our gratitude to everyone at Persea Books: Gabriel Fried, Stefanie Lynne Wortman, Dinah Fried, Rita Lascaro, Fayre Makeig, Karen Braziller, and Michael Braziller.

We would like to recognize the support of the Davis Family Foundation, the Foundation for Contemporary Arts, and the William and Joan Alfond Foundation.

Finally, thanks to the following rights-holders for their permission to reprint the poems in this anthology:

Lindsay Ahl: "Wolf" first appeared on *From the Fishouse*. Reprinted by permission of the author.

Dan Albergotti: "Bad Language" appeared in *The Southeast Review* and appears in *The Boatloads* by Dan Albergotti. Copyright © 2008. Reprinted by permission of BOA Editions.

Kazim Ali: "After I Said It" and "Renunciation" appear in *The Far Mosque* by Kazim Ali. Copyright © 2005. Reprinted by permission of Alice James Books.

Lucy Anderton: "Eve's Sestina for Adam" appeared in *Rattapallax* and in *The Spoken Word Revolution Redux*. Copyright © 2006. Reprinted by permission of the author.

Christian Barter: "Can You" and "Poem" appear in *The Singers I Prefer* by Christian Barter. Copyright © 2005. Reprinted by permission of CavanKerry Press, Ltd. "The Phoenix" appeared in *The Literary Review*. Copyright © 2006. Reprinted by permission of the author.

Curtis Bauer: "I'll Say it This Way" and "A Splinter Becoming a Burning Plank" appear in *Fence Line* by Curtis Bauer. Copyright © 2004. Reprinted by permission of BkMk Press, University of Missouri-Kansas City.

Sherwin Bitsui: "Atlas" appears in *Shapeshift* by Sherwin Bitsui. Copyright © 2003. Reprinted by permission of University of Arizona Press.

Rebecca Black: "Cottonlandia" appeared in *Poetry* and appears in *Cottonlandia* by

Rebecca Black. Copyright © 2005. Reprinted by permission of University of Massachusetts Press.

Adrian Blevins: "Why The Marriage Failed" appeared in *Beloit Poetry Journal*. Copyright © 2005. Reprinted by permission of the author.

Paula Bohince: "Prayer" appeared in *The American Poetry Journal* and appears in *Incident at the Edge of Bayonet Woods* by Paula Bohince. Copyright © 2008. Reprinted by permission of Sarabande Books.

Roger Bonair-Agard: "what the water gave me" and "called: Eurydice" first appeared on *From the Fishouse*. Copyright © 2006. Reprinted by permission of the author.

Shane Book: "Stark Room" first appeared on *From the Fishouse*. Copyright © 2004. "The One" appeared in *Witness*. Copyright © 2004. Reprinted by permission of the author.

Geoffrey Brock: "The State of Virginia after Southampton: 1831" appeared in *The Gettysburg Review*. Copyright © 1999. Reprinted by permission of the author.

Stacey Lynn Brown: "Down South all it takes / to be a church" first appeared on *From the Fishouse* and appears in *Cradle Song* by Stacey Lynn Brown. Copyright © 2009. Reprinted by permission of C&R Press.

Gabrielle Calvocoressi: "A Love Supreme" appeared in *Columbia: A Journal of Literature and Art*. Copyright © 2005. "Late Twentieth Century in the Form of Litany" first appeared on *From the Fishouse*. Copyright © 2006. Reprinted by permission of the author.

Tina Chang: "Invention" appeared in *Callaloo* and "Servitude" appeared in *Cream City Review*. Both appear in *Half-Lit Houses* by Tina Chang. Copyright © 2004. Reprinted by permission of Four Way Books.

Suzanne Cleary: "Echocardiogram" appears in *Trick Pear* by Suzanne Cleary. Copyright © 2007. Reprinted by permission of Carnegie Mellon University Press.

Mark Conway: "Marginalia on Our Bodies" first appeared on *From the Fishouse*. "The Past Described, As a Figure" appeared in *The Paris Review*. Copyright © 2005. Reprinted by permission of the author.

Kyle G. Dargan: "The Battlefield" appears in *The Listening* by Kyle G. Dargan. Copyright © 2004. "Piccolo BLACK ART" first appeared on *From the Fishouse* and appears in *Bouquet of Hungers: Poems* by Kyle G. Dargan. Copyright © 2007. Both reprinted by permission of The University of Georgia Press.

Chad Davidson: "Cleopatra's Bra" appears in *Consolation Miracle* by Chad Davidson. Copyright © 2003. "Diva" appeared in *Hotel Amerika* and appears in *The Last Predicta* by Chad Davidson. Copyright © 2009. Both reprinted by permission of Southern Illinois University Press.

Oliver De La Paz: "Aubade with a Book and the Rattle from a String of Pearls" appeared in *Passages North* and appears in *Furious Lullaby* by Oliver de la Paz. Copyright © 2007. Reprinted by permission of Southern Illinois University Press. "Hello," appears in *Poetry 30: Thirtysomething American Thirtysomething Poets*. Copyright © 2005. Reprinted by permission of the author.

Anthony Deaton: "All Effect" appears in *Rhumb Lines* by Anthony Deaton. Copyright © 2002. Reprinted by permission of the author and Sutton Hoo Press. "An Early Snow and Winter Comes into Kilter" first appeared on *From the Fishouse*. Copyright © 2005. Reprinted by permission of the author.

Diana Marie Delgado: "In the Romantic Longhand of the Night" appeared in *Indiana Review* and "Correspondence" appeared in *The Laurel Review*. Copyright © 2006. Reprinted by permission of the author.

Matthew Dickman: "Love" and "Self-Portrait with Sadness, Wild Turkey, and Denis Johnson" first appeared on *From the Fishouse* and in *Amigos* (Q Ave Press, 2007), and appear in *All-American Poem* by Matthew Dickman. Copyright © 2008. Reprinted by permission of The American Poetry Review.

LaTasha N. Nevada Diggs: "gamelan" first appeared on *From the Fishouse*. Copyright © 2005. Reprinted by permission of the author.

Patrick Donnelly: "Prayer at the Opera" appears in *The Charge* by Patrick Donnelly. Copyright © 2003. Reprinted by permission of Ausable Press.

Camille T. Dungy: "black spoon" appeared in *Brilliant Corners* and "The Preachers Eat Out" appeared in *The Mid-American Review*. Both appear in *What to Eat, What to Drink, What to Leave for Poison* by Camille T. Dungy. Copyright © 2006. Reprinted by permission of Red Hen Press.

Gibson Fay-Leblanc: "Oakland Work Crew" appeared in *The New Republic*. Copyright © 2003. Reprinted by permission of the author.

Monica Ferrell: "The Fire of Despair" appeared in *New England Review* and "Alexander Leaves Babylon" appeared in *Tin House*. Copyright © 2005. Reprinted by permission of the author.

Charles Flowers: "The Way We Were" appeared in *Gulf Coast* and "Aubade" first appeared on *From the Fishouse*. Copyright © 2006. Reprinted by permission of the author.

Sarah Gambito: "Scene: a Loom" appeared in *The Iowa Review* and appears in *Matadora* by Sarah Gambito. Copyright © 2004. Reprinted by permission of Alice James Books.

Ross Gay: "Cousin Drowses on the Flight to Kuwait" and "How to Fall in Love with Your Father" first appeared on *From the Fishouse* and appear in *Against Which* by Ross Gay. Copyright © 2006. Reprinted by permission of CavanKerry Press, Ltd.

Dobby Gibson: "Gone Before" appears in *Polar* by Dobby Gibson. Copyright © 2004. Reprinted by permission of Alice James Books.

Kevin A. González: "Cultural Slut" appeared in *Hotel Amerika* and appears in *Cultural Studies* by Kevin A. González. Copyright © 2009. Reprinted by permission of Carnegie Mellon University Press.

Rigoberto González: "Confession" and "Doppelgänger" first appeared on *From the Fishouse*. Copyright © 2004. Reprinted by permission of the author.

Kevin Goodan: "to crave what the light does crave" and "The first sturdy bee" first appeared on *From the Fishouse* and appear in *Winter Tenor* by Kevin Goodan. Copyright © 2009. Reprinted by permission of the author and Alice James Books.

Stuart Greenhouse: "Cowrie Apostrophe" appeared in *Chelsea* and appears in *What Remains* by Stuart Greenhouse. Copyright © 2005. Reprinted by permission of the author and the Poetry Society of America.

Sarah Gridley: "Under the Veil of Wildness" first appeared on *From the Fishouse*. Copyright © 2006. Reprinted by permission of the author.

Paul Guest: "Questions for Godzilla" appeared in *Hunger Mountain*. Copyright © 2005. Reprinted by permission of the author.

Matthea Harvey: "Ideas Go Only So Far" appears in *Sad Little Breathing Machine* by Matthea Harvey. Copyright © 2004. "The Future of Terror / 11" appeared in a slightly different form in *BOMB Magazine* and appears in *Modern Life* by Matthea Harvey. Copyright © 2007. Both reprinted by permission of Graywolf Press.

James Hoch: "Late Autumn Wasp" appeared in *New England Review* and "The Court of Forgetting" appeared in *Rivendell*. Both appear in *Miscreants* by James Hoch. Copyright © 2007. Reprinted by permission of W.W. Norton & Company, Inc.

Maria Hummel: "Letter to Cain" appeared in *Alligator Juniper*. Copyright © 1997. Reprinted by permission of the author.

Major Jackson: "Selling Out" first appeared on *From the Fishouse* and appears in *Hoops* by Major Jackson. Copyright © 2006. Reprinted by permission of W.W. Norton & Company, Inc. "Leaving Saturn" appears in *Leaving Saturn* by Major Jackson. Copyright © 2001. Reprinted by permission of The University of Georgia Press.

Tyehimba Jess: "leadbelly vs. lomax at the modern language association conference, 1934" first appeared on *From the Fishouse* and appears in *leadbelly* by Tyehimba Jess. Copyright © 2005. Reprinted by permission of Verse Press. "mothafucka" first appeared on *From the Fishouse*. Copyright © 2004. Reprinted by permission of the author.

Amaud Jamaul Johnson: "Burlesque" and "On This Side of Mercy" appear in *Red Summer* by Amaud Jamaul Johnson. Copyright © 2005. Reprinted by permission of Tupelo Press.

Ilya Kaminsky: "Second Ending of the Fairy-Tale" first appeared on *From the Fishouse* and "We Lived Happily During the War" appeared in *Nightsun*. Copyright © 2006. Reprinted by permission of the author. "In Praise of Laughter" appears in *Dancing In Odessa* by Ilya Kaminsky. Copyright © 2004. Reprinted by permission of Tupelo Press.

Gillian Kiley: "The Barrel is Surely Coming Down the Hill" first appeared on *From the Fishouse* and appeared in *Keyhole*. Copyright © 2006. Reprinted by permission of the author.

Ruth Ellen Kocher: "the gigans: v" and "the gigans: xi" first appeared on *From the Fishouse*. Copyright © 2005. Reprinted by permission of the author.

Keetje Kuipers: "The light behind her head, the bright honeycomb of the sky" appeared in *Ellipsis Magazine*. Copyright © 2006. Reprinted by permission of the author.

Rodger Legrand: "Tar the Roof" first appeared on *From the Fishouse* and appears in *Waking Up On a Sinking Boat* by Rodger LeGrand. Copyright © 2008. Reprinted by permission of the author and Pudding House Press.

Dana Levin: "Ars Poetica" and "Quelquechose" appear in *Wedding Day* by Dana Levin. Copyright © 2005. Reprinted by permission of Copper Canyon Press.

Sarah Lindsay: "Cheese Penguin" appears in *Primate Behavior* by Sarah Lindsay. Copyright © 1997. "Lullaby After Midnight" appears in *Mount Clutter* by Sarah Lindsay. Copyright © 2002. Both reprinted by permission of Grove/Atlantic, Inc.

Reb Livingston: "Tonight I Doze" appeared in *Coconut* and appears in *Your Ten Favorite Words* by Reb Livingston. Copyright © 2007. Reprinted by permission of the author and Coconut Books.

Anne Marie Macari: "Little Church" appears in *Gloryland* by Anne Marie Macari. Copyright © 2005. Reprinted by permission of Alice James Books.

Sarah Manguso: "This Might Be Real" appears in *Siste Viator* by Sarah Manguso. Copyright © 2006. Reprinted by permission of Four Way Books.

Sabrina Orah Mark: "Walter B.'s Extraordinary Cousin Arrives for a Visit" first appeared on *From the Fishouse*. Copyright © 2006. Reprinted by permission of the author.

Cate Marvin: "A Windmill Makes a Statement" appeared in *New England Review*. Copyright © 2001. Reprinted by permission of the author.

Adrian Matejka: "Battle Rhyme for the Rhetorical Disenfranchisers" first appeared on *From the Fishouse*. Copyright © 2005. Reprinted by permission of the author. "Understanding Al Green" appears in *The Devil's Garden* by Adrian Matejka. Copyright © 2003. Reprinted by permission of Alice James Books.

Charlotte Matthews: "To The Men Who Mow the County Graveyards" appeared in

The Virginia Quarterly Review and appears in *Still Enough to Be Dreaming* by Charlotte Matthews. Copyright © 2007. Reprinted by permission of Iris Books.

Sebastian Matthews: "What Love Is" appeared in *The Greensboro Review* and appears in *We Generous* by Sebastian Matthews. Copyright © 2007. Reprinted by permission of Red Hen Press.

Leslie Mcgrath: "Corpus" appeared in *Nimrod*. Copyright © 2004. Reprinted by permission of the author.

Michael Mcgriff: "Coos Bay" first appeared on *From the Fishouse*, and appears in *Choke* (Traprock Books, 2006) by Michael McGriff. "Lines Written Before the Day Shift" first appeared on *From the Fishouse*. Both poems appear in *Dismantling the Hills* by Michael McGriff. Copyright © 2008. Reprinted by permission of University of Pittsburgh Press.

Erika Meitner: "Quisiera Declarar" appeared in *Third Coast* and "someone calls" appears in *Snakebird: Thirty Years of Anhinga Poets*. Copyright © 2004. Reprinted by permission of the author.

Sarah Messer: "America, the Hallelujah" appeared in *Indiana Review*. Copyright © 2005. Reprinted by permission of the author. "I Am the Real Jesse James" appeared in *Pierogi Press*, and in *PEN Journal*, and appears in *Bandit Letters* by Sarah Messer. Copyright © 2001. Reprinted by permission of New Issues Poetry & Prose.

Thorpe Moeckel: "Chattooga" appears in *Odd Botany* by Thorpe Moeckel. Copyright © 2002. Reprinted by permission of Silverfish Review Press.

Aimee Nezhukumatathil: "Small Murders" appeared in *Shenandoah* and appears in *Miracle Fruit* by Aimee Nezhukumatathil. Copyright © 2003. Reprinted by permission of Tupelo Press.

Kate Northrop: "The Place above the River" appeared in *32 Poems*. "The Film" first appeared on *From the Fishouse*. Both appear in *Things Are Disappearing Here* by Kate Northrop. Copyright © 2007. Reprinted by permission of Persea Books.

April Ossmann: "Infidelity" appeared in *The Spoon River Poetry Review*. Copyright © 2002. Reprinted by permission of the author.

Eugene Ostashevsky: "Alphabet for Tamar" appears in *Infinite Recursor Or The Bride Of DJ Spinoza* by Eugene Ostashevsky. Copyright © 2005. Reprinted by permission of the author and NY: StudioRADIA / Ugly Duckling Presse.

Gregory Pardlo: "Double Dutch" appeared in *Cave Canem: 2000 Anthology* and appears in *Totem* by Gregory Pardlo. Copyright © 2007. Reprinted by permission of The American Poetry Review.

V. Penelope Pelizzon: "Human Field" appeared in *Web del Sol*; "Seven Penitential Psalms" appeared in *Poetry*; and "To Certain Students" appeared in *The Hudson Review*. Copyright © 2004. Reprinted by permission of the author.

Jon Pineda: "My Sister, Who Died Young, Takes Up the Task" appeared in *Crab Orchard Review* and appears in *The Translator's Diary* by Jon Pineda. Copyright © 2008. Reprinted by permission of New Issues Poetry & Prose.

Hermine Pinson: "Dolores' Blues" appears in *Dolores is Blue/Dolorez is Blues* by Hermine Pinson. Copyright © 2007. Reprinted by permission of the author and Sheep Meadow Press.

John Poch: "Jorie Graham" appeared in *Rivendell*; "Song" and "The Tongue" first appeared on *From the Fishouse*. All three appear in *Poems* by John Poch. Copyright © 2004. Reprinted by permission of Orchises Press.

David Roderick: "Colony" appears in *Blue Colonial* by David Roderick. Copyright © 2006. Reprinted by permission of The American Poetry Review.

Patrick Rosal: "Who Says the Eye Loves Symmetry" and "Uncommon Denominators" appeared in *Uncommon Denominators* (Palanquin Poetry Series, 2001) by Patrick Rosal and appear, along with "The Basque Nose," in *Uprock Headspin Scramble and Dive* by Patrick Rosal. Copyright © 2005. Reprinted by permission of Persea Books.

Steve Scafidi: "Ode to the Perineum" appeared in *The Georgia Review* and with "To Whoever Set My Truck on Fire" in *Sparks from a Nine-Pound Hammer* by Steve Scafidi. Copyright © 2001. Reprinted by permission of Louisiana State University Press.

Ravi Shankar: "Sea Watchers, Oil Paint on Canvas, 1952" first appeared on *From the Fishhouse*. Copyright 2005. "Spangling the Sea" appeared in *The Paris Review* and appears with "Contraction" in *Instrumentality* by Ravi Shankar. Copyright 2005. Reprinted by permission of Cherry Grove Collections.

Matthew Shenoda: "A Prayer for My People" and "For Charles Mingus & That Ever-Living 'Love Chant'" appear in *Somewhere Else* by Matthew Shenoda. Copyright © 2005. Reprinted by permission of Coffee House Press.

Evie Shockley: "à table" first appeared on *From the Fishhouse*, and appears in *a half-red sea* by Evie Shockley. Copyright © 2006. Reprinted by permission of the author and Carolina Wren Press.

Sean Singer: "Ellingtonia" appeared in *Callaloo* and appears in *Discography* by Sean Singer. Copyright © 2002. Reprinted by permission of Yale University Press. "Living On Nothing But Honey And Smoke" first appeared on *From the Fishhouse*. Copyright © 2005. Reprinted by permission of the author.

Tracy K. Smith: "Mangoes" appears in *The Body's Question* by Tracy K. Smith. Copyright © 2003. Reprinted by permission of Graywolf Press.

Laura-Gray Street: "Doorstep Ecologist" first appeared on *From the Fishhouse*. Copyright © 2005. Reprinted by permission of the author.

Jeffrey Thomson: "fabulous ones" appeared in *32 Poems* and on *Verse Daily*. Copyright © 2006. Reprinted by permission of the author. "Imaginary Numbers" appears in *Renovation* by Jeffrey Thomson. Copyright © 2005. Reprinted by permission of Carnegie Mellon University Press.

Brian Turner: "Body Bags" and "Here, Bullet" appeared in *The Georgia Review*. "The Hurt Locker" appeared in *Crab Orchard Review*. All three appear in *Here, Bullet* by Brian Turner. Copyright © 2005. Reprinted by permission of Alice James Books.

Anthony Walton: "Dissidence" appeared in *River Styx* and in *The Vintage Book of African American Poetry*; "Third Shift" appeared in *Prairie Schooner*. Copyright © 2006. Reprinted by permission of the author.

Camille-Yvette Welsch: "Afternoons" first appeared on *From the Fishhouse*. Copyright © 2006. Reprinted by permission of the author.

Gabriel Welsch: "Death and *Taxus*" appeared in *Chautauqua Literary Journal* and appears in *Dirt and All Its Dense Labor* by Gabriel Welsch. Copyright © 2006. Reprinted by permission of WordTech Editions.

Eliot Khalil Wilson: "Last Day with Mayflower" appeared in *The Southern Review* and appears in *The Saint of Letting Small Fish Go* by Eliot Khalil Wilson. Copyright © 2003. Reprinted by permission of Cleveland State University Poetry Center.

Suzanne Wise: "Confession" appears in *The Kingdom of the Subjunctive* by Suzanne Wise. Copyright © 2000. Reprinted by permission of Alice James Books.

Douglas Woodsum: "Melting" first appeared in *The Café Review* and in *Colorado Review*. Copyright © 2005. Reprinted by permission of the author.

About the Editors

CAMILLE T. DUNGY is the author of *What to Eat, What to Drink, What to Leave for Poison* (Red Hen Press, 2006), a finalist for the PEN Center USA 2007 Literary Award and the Library of Virginia 2007 Literary Award. Dungy has received fellowships from organizations including the National Endowment for the Arts, The Virginia Commission for the Arts, Cave Canem, the Bread Loaf Writer's Conference, the Dana Award, and the American Antiquarian Society. She is assistant editor of *Gathering Ground: A Reader Celebrating Cave Canem's First Decade* (University of Michigan Press, 2006). Her second poetry collection, *Suck on the Marrow*, is due from Red Hen Press in 2010. She is currently Associate Professor in the Creative Writing Department at San Francisco State University, and is president of the board of directors of *From the Fishouse*.

MATT O'DONNELL graduated from Holy Cross and earned an MFA in poetry from the University of North Carolina at Greensboro. He is founding Editor & Executive Director of *From the Fishouse*, the online audio archive of emerging poets; Associate Editor of *Bowdoin* magazine at Bowdoin College, where he produces the From the Fishouse Reading Series; and an assistant editor of Poets on Poets, an audio archive of contemporary poets reading Romantic-period poems. His poems have appeared in *Ecotone*, *The Greensboro Review*, *32 Poems*, and elsewhere.

JEFFREY THOMSON is the author of four books of poems, including *Birdwatching in Wartime* (CMU Press, 2009) and *Renovation* (CMU Press, 2005). He has also published a collection of poems translated from the Spanish of Juan Carlos Flores, *Many Ways to Dig a Tunnel* (Green Integer, 2009). He has won fellowships from the National Endowment for the Arts, the Pennsylvania Arts Commission, and was named the 2008 Individual Arts Fellow in the Literary Arts by the Maine Arts Commission. He is an Associate Professor of creative writing at the University of Maine Farmington.

About From the Fishouse

Founded in 2004 by Matt O'Donnell and Camille Dungy, From the Fishouse (www.fishousepoems.org) is a not-for-profit organization that promotes the oral tradition of poetry. Its free online audio archive showcases emerging poets reading their own poems and answering questions about poetry and the writing process. The Fishouse mission is to provide up-and-coming poets an outlet to a wider audience, to provide the public with greater access to authors reading their own work, and to provide an educational resource to students and teachers of contemporary poetry. To date, From the Fishouse has featured thousands of poems by hundreds of contemporary poets.

From the Fishouse takes its name from the writing cabin of the late Lawrence Sargent Hall, who renovated the former codfish-drying shack, dubbing it "Fishouse," and wrote in the space for 50 years. Within the Fishouse, he wrote his Faulkner Award-winning novel *Stowaway* and his O'Henry Award-winning short story "The Ledge," included in *The Best American Short Stories of the Century.*

In 2003, the cabin was rediscovered on Hall's property just as Hall had left it when he died ten years earlier, down to the thesaurus and decanters, photo of his dog, Jack, and even firewood for the stove. With permission from Hall's family, Matt O'Donnell moved the Fishouse to the woods behind his home in Pittston, Maine, to use as his own.